Broadcast:
ABC
WORLD NEWS TONIGHT

4

Shigeru Yamane
Kathleen Yamane

KINSEIDO

Kinseido Publishing Co., Ltd.
3-21 Kanda Jimbo-cho, Chiyoda-ku,
Tokyo 101-0051, Japan

First published 2022 by Kinseido Publishing Co., Ltd.

Foreword

World News Tonight, the flagship news program of the American Broadcast Company, is enjoyed by millions of Americans each evening at 6:30. With its reputation for fair, balanced reporting by a news team who take a personalized look at what's happening around the world and report it with heart, the show is consistently at the top of the evening news ratings.

Since the publication of this textbook series began more than three decades ago, the popular newscasts have become part of the learning experience of tens of thousands of Japanese students, as well. This text is the fourth in our new series, incorporating several changes that we feel enhance the learning experience. As always, we have made every effort to select stories that are not only important but will also make young adults think a little bit harder about the world outside of Japan. This book includes a rich and stimulating cross section of topics, from the situation at the U.S.-Mexico border to the rescue efforts to save sea turtles. Students will meet inspiring heroes like the young poet laureate Amanda Gorman, baseball legend Hank Aaron, and the first group of female Eagle Scouts. The stories will take you all across the U.S. and beyond, from the Suez Canal to Pope Francis' historic trip to Iraq and on to London to learn about Queen Elizabeth's reaction to Prince Harry and Meghan Markle's explosive interview. We feel certain that you will find them all to be as fascinating as we do.

Back in 1987, no one associated with this ABC World News textbook project imagined that the series would have such longevity and touch the lives of so many students. We believe that adopting authentic broadcast news materials for classroom use is a powerful way to build English skills while also helping students to become more knowledgeable about world affairs and to develop the critical thinking skills necessary for all young people in today's increasingly interconnected world. Many of our students also tell us that using the text was good preparation for the TOEFL and TOEIC exams, as well as for job interviews.

To the students using *Broadcast: ABC WORLD NEWS TONIGHT 4*, remember that the skills that you develop using this book can be applied to other news shows, even when the course is over. We sincerely hope that you will challenge yourselves to become more aware of world events and be inspired to follow the news more closely. Happy studying!

January 2022

Kathleen Yamane
Shigeru Yamane

まえがき

近年，日常生活における情報源としてインターネットの活用がますます盛んになってきている。このような高度な情報化社会では，不正確な情報や見方の偏った情報も多くあふれている。学生諸君は，何が本当に自分に役立つ正しい情報か，情報の「質」を見極める能力を身につける必要があるのではないだろうか。

一般的に，テレビニュースからの情報は信頼性が高いといわれている。本書はアメリカの３大ネットワーク（ABC, CBS, NBC）の一つである，ABC放送からのテレビニュース番組を録画し，それを文字化した上で，テキスト用に編集したものである。収録したニュースはアメリカ東部標準時間夕方6時30分から毎日放送されているABC放送の看板ニュース番組*ABC World News Tonight*である。

1948年に始まり，長い歴史を誇るこのABC放送のニュース番組は，ピーター・ジェニングズなど，多くの人気キャスターを生み出してきた。2014年にディビッド・ミューアがアンカーパーソンに抜てきされ，さらに人気が高まった。2015年３月には「アメリカで最も多く視聴されている夕方のニュース番組」となり，アメリカ国内でも絶大な人気を保ちながら，質の高い情報を毎日提供し続けている。

今回も，そのABC放送の看板番組の中から，大学生が学ぶにふさわしい多種多様なニュースを15本厳選し，収録することができた。アメリカ国内のニュースだけではなく，「ローマ教皇，イラクへ平和巡礼の旅」や「メーガン妃のインタビュー発言に揺れる英王室」など，世界のニュースも含まれている。さらに，「ジョージア州の新しい投票法に非難」，「バイデン大統領の歴史的な景気刺激策」など，本書で取り上げた現代社会が抱えるさまざまなトピックを学ぶことを通じて，学生諸君にはニュースの理解を深めながら，自分の意見も持ってもらいたい。また，身近で親しみやすい話題としては，「イースターを楽しく祝う方法」，考えさせる話題としては，「国境に押し寄せる移民たち」など多く収録した。

ニュースを収録した映像は、専用のウェブサイトplus+Media上でストリーミング視聴することができる。ぜひ，学生諸君にはこの映像を繰り返し見てもらいたい。アメリカの家庭で毎日アメリカ人が見ている良質のニュース番組に触れ，信頼できる情報をもとに英語を学んでもらいたい。

本書は1987年に*TV News from the U.S.A.*として始まった。その後，1999年から*ABC World News*として20年間毎年出版され続けた。また2019年には，さまざまな箇所に改良を加え，*Broadcast: ABC WORLD NEWS TONIGHT*と書名を変更し生まれ変わった。アメリカABC放送のニュースを利用した本シリーズは，今回で通算29冊目になり、お陰様で毎回たいへん好評を頂いている。2010年度には外国語教育メディア学会（LET）から，本教材の開発に対して，LET学会賞の「教材開発賞」を受賞する栄誉を頂いた。今後もさらにより良い教材開発の努力を続けていきたい。

最後になったが，テキスト作成に際して毎回大変お世話になっている金星堂のみなさん，今回もこころよく版権を許可してくださったアメリカABC放送に心から感謝の意を表したい。

2022年1月

山根　繁

Kathleen Yamane

Broadcast: ABC WORLD NEWS TONIGHT

4

Table of Contents

News Story 1

Easter Egg Hunt

Before You Watch the News

Air Date: April 4 2021
Duration: 1' 46"

Preview Questions

1. What did the Armstrong family do in their neighborhood for Easter?
——アームストロング家は，イースターに近所で何をしましたか。

2. What was the reaction?
——その反響はどうでしたか。

Warm-up Exercises

A Vocabulary Check: Choose the correct definition for each of the words below.

1. pepper (　)
2. courtesy of (　)
3. stir-crazy (　)
4. ecstatic (　)
5. administer (　)

a. thrilled; overjoyed
b. to fill with; to cover with
c. to give or dispense, especially medical treatment
d. given by; provided by
e. feeling restless, especially as a result of being confined or bored

B Fill in the blanks with appropriate expressions from the Vocabulary Check above. Change the word forms where necessary.

1. The students who volunteered to pick up cans and bottles along the river were given yellow T-shirts, (   ) the local radio station.
2. Everyone was (   ) when our university team won the championship for the second year in a row.
3. The school nurse can provide bandages, but she's not allowed to (   ) drugs.
4. This report is (   ) with spelling mistakes! Do it again!
5. After her accident, Lily went (   ) being stuck in the hospital for two weeks.

News Story [1′ 46″]

L. Davis: Finally, tonight, "America Strong." The family figuring out how to stay socially distant and still celebrate Easter with the neighborhood.

Child: There's an egg, right there.

L. Davis: Peppered all along Pepperwood Avenue in Long Beach, California, you'll find them: 140 colorful wooden Easter eggs all handcrafted and in hiding, courtesy of the Armstrong family, ¹· _____

_____ when the COVID lockdown began last year, right before Easter.

Mother of the Armstrong family: We were going a little stir-crazy on lockdown. We decided to leave eggs ²· _____

_____ for about a five, six-block run of our street.

B. Armstrong, father of the Armstrong family: Good.

L. Davis: Brian Armstrong, a master woodworker, got busy.

B. Armstrong: Oh, yeah, very nice. Whoa.

L. Davis: And the Pepperwood socially-distanced "eggs-travaganza" became a family project.

B. Armstrong: [3.] _____

_____

to put everything together, and you
know, it was a fun process. It kind
of brought us all together.

L. Davis: After days of hard work, each finished egg then wrapped with a note,
reading, "We're the Armstrong family. We're wondering if you would join
us in decorating our community for the holiday?"

Mother: So, the eggs said, hey, put this in your yard, and by the way, there's a
pandemic going on. So, if you need somebody to run to the grocery store
or [4.] _____,
you know, drop us a line.

L. Davis: Many of the neighbors are ecstatic, crediting the family with making
"this world a brighter one!" Another one said, "Love this tradition you
started!" and "Thank you for lifting our spirits up!" An entire family of,
well, good eggs.

Mother: I mean, we're not handing out food or administering vaccines. We're
just putting eggs in yards. But every little bit kind of helps and every
little bit, you know, tiny bit of joy, [5.] _____

_____.

L. Davis: Our thanks to the Armstrongs. I'm Linsey Davis in New York. Have
a great night.

Notes
America Strong「アメリカ・ストロング〈「強くあれ，アメリカ」という心温まるニュース，アメリ
カを元気にしてくれるニュースを紹介するコーナー〉」 **Easter**「イースター；復活祭〈キリストの復活
を祝う祭りで，春分以降，最初の満月の次に来る日曜日に行う〉」 **Long Beach**「ロングビーチ〈カリ
フォルニア州ロサンゼルス市南方の都市で，海辺保養地でもある〉」 **Easter eggs**「イースター・エッ
グ；復活祭の卵〈贈り物・装飾用に使う彩色や模様づけをした卵，または卵形のチョコレートやキャン
ディー。古くから卵は新しい生命の象徴とされている。また，キリストは死の殻を破って復活したとい
われており，雛鳥も卵の殻を破って生まれることから，復活の象徴になったという説がある〉」 **COVID**
「新型コロナウイルス感染症〈= coronavirus disease〉」 **"eggs-travaganza"**「イースター・エッグ
の華やかな祭典（お祭り）〈egg と extravaganza の混成語〉」 **drop ~ a line**「～に連絡する；～に一
報する」 **ecstatic**「この語は語頭に egg を含む "egg-static" に発音上近く聞こえる。他に egg にまつ
わる言葉遊び（だじゃれ）としては "egg-cellent," "egg-streme," "egg-citing" などが考えられる」
crediting ~ with ...「…は～のおかげ」 **good eggs**「良い人たち〈egg には俗語で「～なやつ（人）」
という意味がある〉」

Exercises

A Listen to the CD and fill in the blanks in the text. CD 02

B Mark the following sentences true (T) or false (F) according to the information in the news story.

(　) **1.** The Armstrongs found a way to celebrate Easter with their neighbors while remaining socially distant.

(　) **2.** The wooden Easter egg project is a tradition that started before the pandemic began.

(　) **3.** The project involved several days of hard work, but it brought the Armstrong family closer together.

(　) **4.** A long line of people asked the Armstrongs for help in shopping or picking up mail.

(　) **5.** Members of the community were grateful to the Armstrong family for lifting their spirits up.

(　) **6.** The Armstrong family plans to distribute food to their neighbors next.

C Translate the following Japanese into English. Then listen to the CD and practice the conversation with your partner. CD 03

A: Look at those beautiful wooden Easter eggs! And there are more over there. Drive slowly so we can see them all.

B: They must be from the Armstrongs. **1.** Brian's a master woodworker and _____

_____.

A: I wonder how many they made.

B: I heard it was well over one hundred. **2.** And _____

_____.

A: We're home. Oh, look! There's a colorful package beside the pine tree. It must be from them.

B: What a wonderful thing to do for the neighborhood.

A: And for their family! **3.** _____

_____.

1. ブライアンは木工職人なので，家族のみんなでイースターのために近所の飾り付けをすることにしたのです。

2. そして，困っている近所の人に助けを申し出るため，それら（卵）にメモを残しました。

3. 子どもたちに，人を思いやり，喜びを広める方法を見つけるのを教えることは，とても重要な教訓です。

D **Summary Practice: Fill in the blanks with suitable words beginning with the letters indicated.**

◎ CD 04

The Easter holiday was special this year on Pepperwood Avenue in
($^{1.}$ **L**   ) ($^{2.}$ **B**   ), ($^{3.}$ **c**   ) of the Armstrong family.
Going stir-crazy during ($^{4.}$ **l**   ), the family of Brian
Armstrong, a ($^{5.}$ **m**   ) ($^{6.}$ **w**   ), decided to
brighten up their ($^{7.}$ **c**   ) with ($^{8.}$ **c**   )
wooden Easter eggs. It took the family ($^{9.}$ **t**   ) or ($^{10.}$ **f**   ) days
to prepare the ($^{11.}$ **h**   ) wooden eggs and distribute
them around the ($^{12.}$ **n**   ). There was a note in
each package asking the ($^{13.}$ **e**   ) recipients of the eggs to
($^{14.}$ **d**   ) their ($^{15.}$ **y**   ) with them. They were also
encouraged to get in touch with the Armstrongs if they needed any help
during the ($^{16.}$ **p**   ). A very special family was
($^{17.}$ **c**   ) with lifting the ($^{18.}$ **s**   ) of this
($^{19.}$ **C**   ) community!

E **Discussion: Share your ideas and opinions with your classmates.**

1. How much do you know about Easter? Do an internet search to see what you can learn about this holiday. What do American families typically do for Easter? Are there special foods or activities associated with the day? Look for photos of Easter baskets and Easter candies.

2. Look for stories about ways that people in Japan or other parts of the world tried to spread joy during the lockdown. Were there any special acts in your neighborhood or town?

　英語では，無生物を表す名詞を主語にして表現することがあり，無生物主語が英語表現の大きな特徴となっていることはよく知られている。

— So, ***the eggs said***, hey, put this in your yard, and by the way, there's a pandemic going on.　　　　　　　　　*(Easter Egg Hunt, p.3)*

　上の例では，カラフルな木製のイースターエッグに「これをあなたの庭に置いてください，ところで，パンデミックが起こっています。」と書かれたメッセージが添えられていたという意味なのだが，ここでは "the eggs" が主語になり，動詞は "said" である。

— ***San Francisco*** now ***suing*** its own school district to reopen classes for more than 64,000 students.　　　　　　　*(Reopening Schools, p.16)*

　テレビニュース英語でも，地名，国名，団体名などの無生物が擬人化されて，発言や行動を意味する動詞をとることがよくある。上の例では，「サンフランシスコの教員組合は現在，64,000 人以上の生徒の授業を再開するために自分の学区を訴えています。」という意味になるが，地名の "San Francisco" は擬人化された主語で，動詞は sue になっている。

— President Biden declaring to the world ***America is*** back to work with our allies, ...　　　　　　　　　　　　*(America is Back, p.28)*
— ***Daylight revealing*** a town torn to pieces.　*(Coast-to-Coast Storms, p.34)*
— ***Buckingham Palace is*** now ***responding*** after that interview with Harry and Meghan, including those accusations involving race.
　　　　　　　　　　　　　　　　　　(Queen: Family Saddened, p.71)
— ***Sources say*** Prince Charles, the future king, believes diversity is Britain's greatest strength...　　　*(Queen: Family Saddened, p.72)*
— ..., ***DHS says*** it expects the surge to continue, ...
　　　　　　　　　　　　　　　　　　　(Crisis at the Border, p.90)
— ***Sources say*** the number of unaccompanied children under the age of 18 in Border Patrol custody jumped 25% in just the last week.
　　　　　　　　　　　　　　　　　　　(Crisis at the Border, p.91)

News Story 2

Youngest Inaugural Poet

Air Date: January 20 2021
Duration: 2' 06"

Preview Questions

1. Who is Amanda Gorman? Why is she in the news?
——アマンダ・ゴーマンとは誰ですか。なぜ彼女はニュースになっているのですか。

2. What is her message to America?
——彼女はアメリカへどのようなメッセージを伝えていますか。

Warm-up Exercises

A Vocabulary Check: Choose the correct definition for each of the words below.

1. weather (　)   **a.** to resolve or settle
2. shatter (　)   **b.** a small, cozy space
3. reconcile (　)   **c.** to endure; to survive
4. nook (　)   **d.** to materialize; to come into view
5. emerge (　)   **e.** to destroy; to break

B Fill in the blanks with appropriate expressions from the Vocabulary Check above. Change the word forms where necessary.

1. My favorite teapot was (   ) during the earthquake.
2. If you and Pete talk honestly, you'll be able to (   ) your differences.
3. My favorite place to read is a pleasant (   ) beside the fireplace.
4. Meg is upset about losing her job, but she'll be okay soon. She has (   ) worse.
5. A beautiful full moon (   ) from behind the clouds.

News Story [2′ 06″]

D. Muir: Finally tonight here, she moved millions with her words. The youngest inaugural poet ever in U.S. history.

She is the 22-year-old poet seen by the nation today. Amanda Gorman from Los Angeles. Her mother right there. Invited by First Lady Jill Biden to read a poem that ¹· _____ _____. She calls it "The Hill We Climb."

A. Gorman, American Poet: We've weathered and witnessed a nation that isn't ₁₀ broken, but simply unfinished. We, the successors of a country and a time where a skinny black girl descended from slaves and ²· _____ _____ can dream of becoming president, only to find herself reciting for one.

D. Muir: The young poet saying she stayed up all night writing the poem after ₁₅ watching the attack on the Capitol.

A. Gorman: We've seen a force that would shatter our nation, ³· _____ _____. Would destroy our country if it meant delaying democracy. And this effort very nearly succeeded. But while democracy can be periodically delayed, it can never be permanently ₂₀ defeated.

D. Muir: Gorman is the first National
Youth Poet Laureate. And today,

4. _____

_____, too.

A. Gorman: We will rebuild, reconcile,
and recover. And every known
nook of our nation and every corner called our country, our people
diverse and beautiful, will emerge battered and beautiful. When day
comes, we step out of the shade aflame and unafraid. The new dawn
blooms as we free it. 5. _____,
if only we're brave enough to see it. If only we're brave enough to be it.

5

10

D.Muir: Amanda Gorman. Remember her name. And she'll be on with Robin
first thing in the morning on *GMA*. Good night.

Notes **inaugural poet**「大統領就任式の詩人〈大統領の就任式に初めて詩人が招かれたのは 1961 年のジョン・F・ケネディ大統領の就任式で,その後もときおり詩人が招かれている〉」 **The Hill We Climb**「われらが登る丘」 **the attack on the Capitol**「連邦議会議事堂への襲撃〈2021 年 1 月 6 日にドナルド・トランプ前大統領の支持者たちが 2020 年の大統領選での選挙不正を訴えて暴動を起こした事件〉」 **National Youth Poet Laureate**「全米青年桂冠詩人〈2017 年に創設された優れた若手詩人に贈られる賞で,アマンダさんはその第 1 回受賞者となった〉」 **battered**「打ちのめされて;ぼろぼろになって」 **new dawn blooms**「新しい(時代の)夜明けが来る」 **Robin**「= Robin René Roberts〈ABC 放送の番組 *GMA* のアンカーパーソン〉」 **GMA**「= *Good Morning America*〈ABC で放送されている朝の情報番組〉」

大統領就任式に初めて詩人を招いた 1961 年のケネディ元大統領に続いて，1993 年と 1997 年にはクリントン元大統領，2009 年と 2013 年にはオバマ元大統領の就任式に詩人が招かれた。アマンダ・ゴーマンさんは，大統領就任式で詩を朗読した 6 人目の詩人で，しかも最年少での抜てきであった。ジル・バイデン大統領夫人が彼女の詩を気に入り，ゴーマンさんが今回の大役を務めることとなった。

ゴーマンさんはバイデン大統領の就任式のために「われらが登る丘」(The Hill We Climb) を書き下ろした。バイデン氏が就任式の準備を進めていた 2020 年末，彼女は詩の創作に取りかかったが，実際には，大統領就任式直前に起きた連邦議会議事堂 (the Capitol) の襲撃・占拠事件に衝撃を受け，詩を一気に完成させたという。

ロサンゼルスに生まれたゴーマンさんは，双子の姉妹として英語教師のシングルマザーに育てられた。幼少時には / r / の音を発音できない言語障がいがあったものの，母親の励ましのもと，それを克服して詩作の道に進んだという。今回の詩の中でも "We will rebuild, reconcile, and recover." と，/ r / 音で始まる頭韻を見事に駆使している。詩の一節に「やせた黒人の女の子 (a skinny black girl) が大統領を夢見る」とあるように，ハーバード大学を卒業したばかりの彼女は将来，大統領に立候補する自身の夢を告白した。

After You Watch the News

Exercises

A Listen to the CD and fill in the blanks in the text.　　　　　　　◎ CD 05

B Multiple Choice Questions

1. Which of the following statements about Gorman is true?

   a. She was invited by the president to recite her poem.

   b. She can dream of becoming president of the U.S.

   c. She was the youngest person to attend the Inaugural.

2. Which American problem does Gorman *NOT* refer to in her poem?

    a. slavery

    b. single motherhood

    c. the California wildfires

3. Amanda Gorman worked on "The Hill We Climb"

    a. in order to become rich and famous.

    b. mainly to tell people the story of her life.

    c. all night after the shocking attack on the Capitol.

4. In her poem, Gorman suggests that

    a. the attack on the Capitol left the U.S. battered forever.

    b. the U.S. has successfully recovered due to its diversity.

    c. there is hope that the U.S. will be able to find unity someday.

C Translate the following Japanese into English. Then listen to the CD and practice the conversation with your partner. ◎ CD 06

A: There she is! Come on, Jim. It's time for Amanda's poem.

B: I thought inaugural poets were always famous old people.

A: They usually are. ¹· _____

_____

_____.

B: We know she's amazing, but how did they ever find her?

A: ²· _____

_____.

B: Cool! Amanda worked so hard preparing for this. I know she'll do a great job.

A: ³· _____

_____.

1. アマンダは、大統領就任式で詩を朗読した史上最年少の人です。

2. ファーストレディーがアマンダに詩の朗読を依頼したのです。

3. 彼女には、言葉で人を感動させる本物の才能があります。

D Summary Practice: Fill in the blanks with suitable words beginning with the letters indicated.

⊙ CD 07

One of the highlights of the presidential inauguration held on January 20th was the poem recited by (¹· **A**   ) (²· **G**   ). At (³· **t**   )-(⁴· **t**   ) years of age, Gorman was the youngest (⁵· **i**   ) (⁶· **p**   ) ever, but her words (⁷· **m**   ) millions of people. In "The (⁸· **H**   ) We (⁹· **C**   )" the young poet described herself as a (¹⁰· **s**   ) black girl descended from (¹¹· **s**   ) who could now dream of becoming president, and found herself (¹²· **r**   ) for one. She reacted to the (¹³· **a**   ) on the (¹⁴· **C**   ), calling it "a (¹⁵· **f**   ) that would (¹⁶· **s**   ) our (¹⁷· **n**   )" but urging Americans to "rebuild, (¹⁸· **r**   ), and recover." Her call for (¹⁹· **u**   ) concluded with a challenge to all Americans to be (²⁰· **b**   ) enough to see the (²¹· **l**   ), and "brave enough to be it."

E Discussion: Share your ideas and opinions with your classmates.

1. Amanda Gorman received a great deal of attention for her reading at the inauguration. Do an internet search and see what she has been doing since that time.

2. Find the full poem "The Hill We Climb" and read it out loud. What are some of the powerful images in the poem? What do you notice about the sounds and rhythm?

3. What is the role of the inaugural poets? Who are some other former inaugural poets? Share your findings with the class.

　ゴーマンさんの詩の朗読を聞くと，太字・斜体で示した音節を強く読んでいることに気がつく。英語ではこの強く発音される強音節が，弱く発音される弱音節を挟んで一定のペースで繰り返される。詩ではこの傾向がさらに顕著で，リズミカルで心地よく聞こえる。

— We've **wéath**ered and **wit**nessed a **ná**tion that isn't **bró**ken, but **sim**ply un**fín**ished. **Wé**, the suc**cés**sors of a **cóun**try and a **tíme** where a **skín**ny **bláck gírl** de**scénd**ed from **sláves**...

(Youngest Inaugural Poet, p.8)

　一般的に，品詞の中で強く発音されてアクセントを受けるのは一般動詞，名詞，形容詞，副詞など，センテンス内で重要な意味内容を担う内容語（content word）である。その他，アクセントが置かれるのは疑問詞（文頭で使われる who, what, when, where など），指示代名詞（this, that, these, those），所有代名詞（mine, yours, hers, theirs など），句動詞中の副詞辞（look <u>forward</u> to, take <u>off</u> など），否定辞（not, isn't, can't など）である。反対に，アクセントを受けないのは前置詞，冠詞，助動詞，接続詞，代名詞，関係代名詞など，主に文法的な関係を示す機能語（function word）である。上記の詩では "We, the successors…" の代名詞 "We" は，意味を強調するためにアクセントを置いて発音されている。

— Would **de**stroy our country if it meant **de**laying **de**mocracy. And this effort very nearly succeeded. But while **de**mocracy can be periodically **de**layed, it can never be permanently **de**feated.

(Youngest Inaugural Poet, p.8)

　また，上の例では，/dɪ/ で始まる音節が繰り返されて頭韻を踏んでいるため，テンポよく聞こえ，直接的に聞き手に訴えかける印象が強くなる。

Reopening Schools

Air Date: February 4 2021
Duration: 2' 14"

Before You Watch the News

Preview Questions

1. What has the head of the CDC said about reopening schools?
——CDC（アメリカ疫病管理予防センター）の責任者は、学校の再開についてどのような発言をしていますか。

2. How do many teachers feel about that decision?
——教員の多くはその決定をどのように感じていますか。

Warm-up Exercises

A Vocabulary Check: Choose the correct definition for each of the words below.

1. face-off (　　)

2. outrage (　　)

3. negotiation (　　)

4. standstill (　　)

5. transmission (　　)

a. extreme anger

b. discussion aimed at reaching an agreement

c. the act of spreading; the act of passing on to others

d. conflict; direct confrontation

e. complete stop; halt

B Fill in the blanks with appropriate expressions from the Vocabulary Check above. Change the word forms where necessary.

1. The (　　　　　　) between the two competitors has become increasingly tense.
2. Traffic came to a (　　　　　　) while the deer crossed the road.
3. The ban on e-cigarettes is currently under (　　　　　　).
4. Many reacted with (　　　　　　) when the manager accused of fraud was pronounced innocent.
5. The (　　　　　　) of local culture to the next generation is considered an important responsibility of the elderly.

News Story [2′ 14″]

D. Muir: Next here to the growing debate across this country over opening more of our nation's schools. The new head of the CDC saying the science now shows that, with proper mitigation, masks and distancing, that we can open schools without vaccinating all teachers first. **1.** _____ _____, and many teachers and teachers' unions are still fighting it. ABC's Kayna Whitworth, from California tonight.

Protesters: Open schools now!

K. Whitworth: Tonight, a face-off across the U.S. over students' safe return to in-person learning.

D. Herrera, City Attorney, San Francisco: Not a single San Francisco public school student has set foot in their classroom in 327 days.

K. Whitworth: In California, **2.** _____ _____ have been closed nearly a year, outrage is growing.

T. Bettles, parent: And if anyone thinks a six- or seven-year-old can learn to read and write over Zoom, they're kidding themselves.

K. Whitworth: San Francisco now suing its own school district to reopen classes for more than 64,000 students. ^{3.} _____ _____ to get K-8 students safely back in the classroom, part of President Biden's 100-day plan, including an additional $130 billion in COVID relief funding to help schools. But from Chicago...

B. Imbus, teacher: Save our lives!

Protesters: Save lives!

K. Whitworth: ...to Albuquerque, union negotiations at a standstill. Students and parents pitted against teachers who say they should be vaccinated *4.* _____.

B. Imbus: We're angry that they're gonna try to force us back into in-person school when it's not safe.

K. Whitworth: The new CDC director making headlines when she said the science now shows ^{5.} _____ _____ without vaccinating teachers. Overnight, she was pressed to defend her comments.

Dr. R. Walensky, Director, CDC: There is not a lot of transmission that is happening in schools when there is masking, when there is distancing, de-densification of the classroom, ventilation, contact tracing, hand-washing.

K. Whitworth: And, David, part of President Biden... President Biden's plan with this extra funding is to provide schools with the resources they need, like PPE, proper ventilation and testing. But, David, some teachers we spoke with maintain ^{6.} _____ until they're vaccinated.

Notes **CDC**「アメリカ疾病管理予防センター〈= Centers for Disease Control and Prevention 感染症対策など人々の健康と安全の保護を主導するアメリカの政府機関でジョージア州アトランタにある〉」 **mitigation**「緩和策〈感染拡大などの危険を緩和するための策〉」 **The new head of the CDC saying …, that we can open schools without vaccinating all teachers first.**「〈文法的には，この that は不要〉」 **in-person learning**「対面式の学習」 **set foot in ~**「～に足を踏み入れる」 **kidding themselves**「現実を甘く見ている；考えが甘い」 **K-8 students**「幼稚園 (kindergarten) から 8 年生までの生徒〈アメリカでは K-12 が義務教育とされており，小学校 1 年から 12 年まで，中学・高校になっても学年を 1 年から数えなおさず順に数える。8 年生は日本の中学 2 年生にあたる〉」 **COVID relief funding**「新型コロナウイルス感染症救済資金」 **Albuquerque**「アルバカーキ〈ニューメキシコ州最大の都市〉」 **pitted against ~**「～と対立している」 **making headlines**「大きな話題になった」 **was pressed**「迫られた」 **de-densification**「低密度化〈教室内の生徒数を減らすこと〉」 **contact tracing**「（感染病の）接触者追跡」 **PPE**「個人用防護具〈= Personal Protective Equipment ガウン，手袋，高性能マスク，ゴーグルなど感染を防止するための装具〉」

After　You Watch the News

Exercises

A Listen to the CD and fill in the blanks in the text.　　◎ CD 08

B Mark the following sentences true (T) or false (F) according to the information in the news story.

(　) **1.** The CDC director claims that her decision to open schools without fully vaccinating teachers is based on science.

(　) **2.** Some parents in California are outraged because they want their children to be vaccinated.

(　) **3.** Students in San Francisco have been studying online for over a year because the public schools have been closed.

(　) **4.** President Biden's plan supports getting students back to school as quickly as possible, but safely.

(　) **5.** Teachers in Albuquerque do not want to return to school without increased funding for resources.

(　) **6.** Dr. Walensky has had to defend her comments to many teachers and teachers' unions.

C Translate the following Japanese into English. Then listen to the CD and practice the conversation with your partner. CD 09

A: Can you believe what the CDC director said yesterday?

B: That it's time to get the students back to school? Hooray!

A: Everyone agrees with that. **1.** But _____
_____?

B: **2.** Actually, _____
_____.

A: Well, my sister is a teacher, and she is outraged. It's not easy to control six- and seven-year olds, you know.

B: **3.** _____
_____?

A: Nope. Maybe he should reconsider the plan. Our kids need to get back to school.

1. でも，先生たちが先に予防接種を受けるべきだと思いませんか。

2. 実は，適切な換気とマスクがあれば，学校での感染は問題ないようです。

3. バイデン大統領の 100 日計画には、予防接種に関して何か含まれていなかったかのですか。

D **Summary Practice: Fill in the blanks with suitable words beginning with the letters indicated.**

⊙ CD 10

It's the teachers' (¹· **u**   ) vs. the parents in the latest
(²· **f**   )-(³· **o**   ) regarding a return to (⁴· **i**   )-(⁵· **p**   ) learning.
The debate follows comments by current CDC Director Rochelle Walensky
asserting that it is safe for schools to (⁶· **r**   ) even without
(⁷· **v**   ) all of the teachers. Her comments prompted
(⁸· **o**   ) from teachers, some claiming that they would not
return to school until they had received a vaccination. Meanwhile,
frustration is growing among parents in the state of
(⁹· **C**   ), where most of its 10,000 (¹⁰· **p**   ) schools
have been closed for almost a year. Sentiments are so strong that
(¹¹· **S**   ) (¹²· **F**   ) is even suing its school (¹³· **d**   ).
President Biden's (¹⁴· **o**   )-(¹⁵· **h**   )-day plan offers an
additional $130 (¹⁶· **b**   ) in financial relief to help schools reopen
safely, but that does not include vaccinations for teachers. According to
Director Walensky, (¹⁷· **s**   ) shows that there is not a lot of
(¹⁸· **t**   ) in schools as long as good
(¹⁹· **v**   ), social (²⁰· **d**   ) and
(²¹· **m**   ) are prioritized. Tonight, the fight continues.

E **Discussion: Share your ideas and opinions with your classmates.**

1. Do an internet search to find out how schools in another country of your choice are educating students during the pandemic. Try to find information about elementary schools as well as high schools and universities. Share your findings with the class.
2. What has been the situation of the schools in your area during the pandemic? Have you personally experienced Zoom or other online classes? What are the good and bad points? How did your daily routine change?
3. What safety measures have been taken at your school during the pandemic? Do most students feel they are reasonable?

　書きことばの新聞英語の「見出し」では，be 動詞が省略されることはよく知られている。テレビニュース英語では，特に冒頭の箇所で，何についてのニュースであるか，そのトピックを告げるときに頻繁に be 動詞が省略される。新聞英語の「見出し」的な役割を果たしている。（∧）は be 動詞が省略されている箇所を示している。

— San Francisco ∧ now suing its own school district to reopen classes
　　for more than 64,000 students.　　　　　　　　*(Reopening Schools, p.16)*

　上記の例では，∧の箇所に "is" が入ると思われるが，これを省略することによって，箇条書き的な文体になり，情報をきびきびと伝えることができる。

— ..., union negotiations ∧ at a standstill.　　　*(Reopening Schools, p.16)*
— The new CDC director ∧ making headlines when she said the
　　science now shows...　　　　　　　　　　　　*(Reopening Schools, p.16)*
— Overseas now, Pope Francis ∧ making history.

　　　　　　　　　　　　　　　　　　　　　　(Pope's Historic Trip, p.22)

— The Pope ∧ celebrating mass at an outdoor stadium in front of
　　thousands of worshippers, ...　　　　　　　*(Pope's Historic Trip, p.22)*
— Biden ∧ vowing to rebuild alliances and trust.　*(America is Back, p.28)*
— A teenager ∧ killed while hiding in the basement with his family.

　　　　　　　　　　　　　　　　　　　　　(Coast-to-Coast Storms, p.33)

— This hotel ∧ ripped apart.　　　　　　　　　*(Coast-to-Coast Storms, p.33)*
— Some 30 people ∧ hurt.　　　　　　　　　　*(Coast-to-Coast Storms, p.34)*
— ..., the nation ∧ celebrating the life of Hall of Famer Hank Aaron.

　　　　　　　　　　　　　　　　(Hank Aaron: Baseball Legend, p.39)

— The group Sea Turtle, Inc. ∧ among the groups ∧ helping.

　　　　　　　　　　　　　　(Turtles Rescued from the Cold, p.45)

Pope's Historic Trip

Air Date: March 7 2021
Duration: 1' 54"

Preview Questions

1. What was the purpose of the Pope's trip?
　——教皇の旅の目的は何でしたか。

2. How was his visit received?
　——彼の訪問はどのように受け止められましたか。

Warm-up Exercises

A Vocabulary Check: Choose the correct definition for each of the words below.

1. devastated （　）
2. groundbreaking （　）
3. urgent （　）
4. bolster （　）
5. beleaguered （　）

a. requiring immediate action or attention
b. to support or strengthen
c. in a very difficult situation
d. destroyed; ruined
e. pioneering; innovative

B Fill in the blanks with appropriate expressions from the Vocabulary Check above. Change the word forms where necessary.

1. I've got a lot to do this morning, but if it's (   ), I can meet you at 10.
2. The (   ) research on Alzheimer's is giving hope to thousands of patients.
3. The coastline of the village was (   ) by the recent typhoon.
4. Kim looks miserable since her sister moved away. What can we do to (   ) her spirits?
5. The (   ) health care workers requested assistance from medical students.

News Story [1' 54"]

L. Davis: Overseas now, Pope Francis making history. The Pontiff in northern Iraq today, calling for unity and forgiveness for Muslim extremists as he visited several churches destroyed by ISIS. The Pope celebrating mass at an outdoor stadium in front of thousands of worshippers, many of them maskless. This is the Pontiff's ¹· _____ _____. ABC's senior foreign correspondent Ian   10
Pannell is in Iraq.

I. Pannell: Tonight, a huge open air mass for Pope Francis in Iraq. Greeted by thousands of ecstatic worshippers, gathered together in a sports stadium, despite fears of rising COVID infections.

  ². _____,   15
incredible for Christians, Yazidis, Arabs and Kurds. In a country devastated by war and terror, the Pope is here, on a pilgrimage of peace.

This was his last stop on a groundbreaking trip that Francis has tried to make for years. He released a dove, symbolizing peace, saying Iraq would remain in his heart. Earlier, he visited the war-torn ruins of Mosul. It's   20 where Abu Bakr al-Baghdadi declared the caliphate of ISIS, and he threatened, "3. _____ _____." But instead, on an historic day, Rome, the Pope, came to Mosul on a pilgrimage of peace.

In the ruins of four churches occupied by ISIS, he made an urgent plea for coexistence, praying for the souls of the thousands and thousands killed in the city. Qaraqosh is the country's largest Christian town, but ISIS drove them out, and today, 4. _____ _____. With joy and relief, the faithful greeted the Pope, who's trying to bolster this ancient, beleaguered community.

Despite the very real threats and fears for the Pope's safety, this trip has been a huge success. 5. _____, Iraqis are just desperate for a better tomorrow, but very real problems and dangers remain here.

Notes **The Pontiff**「ローマ教皇〈ローマ・カトリック教会の最高指導者〉」 **Muslim extremists**「イスラム過激派」 **ISIS**「アイシス；イスラム国〈= Islamic State of Iraq and Syria イラクとシリアで発生したイスラム過激派組織で，各地でテロ攻撃を仕掛け，世界を恐怖に陥れた〉」 **senior foreign correspondent**「上席海外特派員（記者）」 **Yazidis**「ヤジディ教徒〈イラク北部などに住むクルド人の一部が信仰する民族宗教の信者〉」 **Kurds**「クルド人〈トルコ，イラク，イラン，シリアの国境地帯に住む民族〉」 **pilgrimage of peace**「平和への巡礼」 **Mosul**「モスル〈イラク北部の都市で，イラク政府がアメリカを中心とした連合軍の支援を受けて過激派組織のイスラム国（ISIS）からの解放を2017年に宣言した〉」 **Abu Bakr al-Baghdadi**「アブ・バクル・アル・バグダディ〈イスラム国（ISIS）の元指導者で，2019年10月，シリア北西部で行われた米軍事作戦で死亡した〉」 **caliphate**「カリフの地位；支配権〈イスラム世界の宗教と政治両方の権威を持つ最高指導者，支配者〉」 **Qaraqosh**「カラコシュ〈イラク北部の都市。2014年，ISISに占領され家屋や教会などの主要な施設が破壊されたが，2年後の2016年に解放された〉」 **the faithful**「（キリスト教の）忠実な信者たち」

Background of the News

　世界で約 13 億人の信者を抱えるローマ・カトリック教会のトップ，フランシスコ教皇（Pope Francis）は，総本山バチカンを離れ 2021 年 3 月 5 日〜 8 日，イラクを訪れた。歴代ローマ教皇で初めてのイラク訪問となる。教皇の外遊は，2019 年 11 月の訪日以来およそ 1 年 3 カ月ぶりとなった。

　イラクはその人口 4 千万人弱の大半がイスラム教徒（Muslim）であるが，多数派のシーア派と少数派スンニ派との宗派対立に長年苦しんできた。2021 年 3 月 7 日付の「日経速報ニュースアーカイブ」によると，キリスト教徒はもともと圧倒的少数派ではあるものの，イラク戦争が開戦した 2003 年の約 140 万人から 25 万人程度まで減ったとされる。さらに，2014 年に台頭したスンニ派のイスラム過激派（Muslim extremists）であるイスラム国（ISIS）はキリスト教徒を迫害し，信者の国外亡命が相次いだ。

　教皇は，2014 〜 2017 年に ISIS が拠点とした主要都市モスル（Mosul）で，宗教間の無理解や対立を乗り越えることと，異なる背景を持つ人々の共生（coexistence）と融和の重要性を訴えた。

　教皇はユダヤ教，キリスト教，イスラム教の共通の「信仰の父」であるアブラハムの生誕地とされるウルで諸宗教の代表者との集会にも参加した。コロナ禍の中，高齢の教皇が今回イラクを訪問したのは，この地が，教皇が力を入れる「和解と対話」をアピールするには絶好の場所だったからとの見解もある。

After　You Watch the News

Exercises

A Listen to the CD and fill in the blanks in the text.　 CD 11

B Multiple Choice Questions

1. What is **NOT** mentioned about the Pope's historic trip?

   a. He celebrated mass in an outdoor stadium.

   b. He asked for forgiveness for the Muslim extremists.

   c. He prayed for an end to the COVID pandemic.

2. The Pope's visit to Iraq is being called historic because

   a. it was a pilgrimage of peace to a war-torn country.

   b. it was his first trip abroad since the pandemic began.

   c. both *a* and *b*

3. What happened in Mosul?

    a. The Pope prayed together with Muslim extremists and ecstatic Christian worshippers.

    b. An ISIS leader declared that they would occupy Rome, but the Pope visited them from Rome.

    c. The Pontiff released a dove as a symbol of peace on the first stop of his long-awaited trip.

4. The Christians in Qaraqosh

    a. number only half what they were.

    b. were driven out to the largest Christian town.

    c. bolstered the Pope on his visit to their ancient town.

C Translate the following Japanese into English. Then listen to the CD and practice the conversation with your partner.   CD 12

A: Did you hear that the Pope is in Iraq?

B: No! Isn't that dangerous? What about the Muslim terrorists?

A: 1. _____

_____ .

B: It wasn't so long ago that the ISIS caliphate declared they were going to occupy Rome.

A: Well, now Rome has come to them! 2. And _____

_____ .

B: That must be hard for the Christians there to hear. 3. _____

_____

_____ .

A: For Pope Francis, this is a true pilgrimage of peace.

1. 実際に脅威はあったのですが，教皇は何年も前からこの旅をしたいと思っていたのです。
2. そして，教皇は過激派を許すことさえ求めています。
3. 教会は破壊され、何千人もの人々が家を追われました。

Summary Practice: Fill in the blanks with suitable words beginning with the letters indicated.

A sports ($^{1.}$ s   ) was the site of a huge open air ($^{2.}$ m   )
celebrated by ($^{3.}$ P   ) ($^{4.}$ F   ) for an audience of thousands
of ($^{5.}$ e   ) ($^{6.}$ w   ). The Pope's
($^{7.}$ h   ) trip to Iraq, a region ($^{8.}$ d   ) by
($^{9.}$ w   ) and terror, is one that he has been trying to make for years. The
Pope brought a message of ($^{10.}$ p   ) and ($^{11.}$ f   ),
even forgiving the ($^{12.}$ M   ) ($^{13.}$ e   ) as he
visited ($^{14.}$ c   ) that had been destroyed by ISIS. As a part of
his ($^{15.}$ p   ) of peace, the Pontiff released a symbolic
($^{16.}$ d   ), promising to keep Iraq in his ($^{17.}$ h   ). In spite of fears
about the Pope's ($^{18.}$ s   ) and the spread of the COVID
($^{19.}$ i   ), the Pope's visit and pleas for ($^{20.}$ c   )
brought joy to the people he met in Iraq.

E **Discussion: Share your ideas and opinions with your classmates.**

1. What do you know about Pope Francis? In what ways is he different from other popes? Do an internet search and share your findings with your classmates.

2. A number of different ethnic and religious groups are mentioned in this news story. Choose one and see what you can learn about them.

3. How much do you know about ISIS? What do they aim to accomplish? In addition to the destruction mentioned in the news story, what else have they done to promote their goals?

America is Back

Air Date: February 4 2021
Duration: 1′ 41″

Preview Questions

1. What promise did President Biden make in his foreign policy speech?

——バイデン大統領が外交政策演説で掲げた約束とは何ですか。

2. What did he say about Russia?

——ロシアについてどのような発言をしましたか。

Warm-up Exercises

A **Vocabulary Check: Choose the correct definition for each of the words below.**

1. stern (   )

2. aggressive (   )

3. alliance (   )

4. adversary (   )

5. morale (   )

a. confidence; spirits

b. opponent; enemy

c. serious; strict

d. partnership; association

e. confrontational; hostile

B Fill in the blanks with appropriate expressions from the Vocabulary Check above. Change the word forms where necessary.

1. That dog is quite (   ). Be sure to keep your distance.

2. Wow! My favorite tennis player just beat her long-time (   )!

3. When Ms. Taylor gives us that (   ) look, we know we have to be quiet.

4. (   ) has been pretty low lately. Let's plan something fun to cheer everyone up.

5. Once the (   ) is approved, the two organizations can begin collaborating on some new projects.

News Story [1′ 41″]

D. Muir: President Biden, meanwhile, with a stern warning for Russia tonight. During his first major foreign policy speech, the president saying, quote, "The days of the United States rolling over in the face of Russia's aggressive actions are over." President Biden declaring to the world America is back to work with our allies, but **1.** _____

_____ delivered to those who work

at the State Department. Here's our senior White House correspondent, Mary Bruce, tonight.

M. Bruce: 2. _____

_____, President Biden with a promise.

President J. Biden: America is back. Diplomacy is back.

M. Bruce: It's a sharp departure from the policies of former President Trump, who shrank the State Department **3.** _____.
Biden vowing to rebuild alliances and trust.

President J. Biden: Leading with diplomacy means standing shoulder-to-shoulder with our allies and **4.** _____

_____.

M. Bruce: Biden, today, taking steps to raise the cap on refugees allowed into the U.S. from 15,000 to 125,000, and ending U.S. support for Saudi Arabia's military campaign in Yemen. He's also putting adversaries like Russia on notice.

5

President J. Biden: The days of the United States rolling over in the face of Russia's aggressive actions, interfering with our elections, cyberattacks, poisoning its citizens, are over.

10

M. Bruce: Earlier, speaking to State Department employees, the president saying he's got their backs.

Now morale at the State Department has also taken a big hit during these last four years. The president today telling staffers **5.** _____ _____. It's a message that we're told tonight was well received. But members of the diplomatic corps are also eager to see how the president fulfills these promises going forward. David?

15

Notes rolling over「屈する」 **State Department**「国務省」 **senior White House correspondent**「ホワイトハウス担当上席記者」 **Leading with ~**「~を主導する」 **raise the cap on ~**「~の上限を引き上げる」 **military campaign**「軍事作戦」 **putting ~ on notice**「~に注意を促している；~に通告している」 **got their backs**「彼らを支援する；彼らの味方だ」 **taken a big hit**「大きく低下した；大きな打撃を受けた」 **diplomatic corps**「外交団（国務省の職員たち）」

After ▏ You Watch the News

Exercises
A **Listen to the CD and fill in the blanks in the text.**　　 CD 14

B Multiple Choice Questions

1. When he says "America is back" Biden suggests that the U.S.
   a. will require its allies to lead with diplomacy.
   b. will rebuild and strengthen alliances with its adversaries.
   c. will return to policies in place before Donald Trump became president.

2. Which of the following is **NOT** part of President Biden's plan?
   a. dealing strictly with Russia
   b. working closely with U.S. allies
   c. doubling the number of refugees allowed into the U.S.

3. According to the news story, employees of the U.S. State Department
   a. were at the heart of U.S. policy for the past four years.
   b. had a positive reaction to President Biden's speech.
   c. have been put on notice that they need to build morale.

4. Which of the following best describes foreign policy in the period before Biden became president?
   a. weak on Russian aggression and making the State Department weaker
   b. strengthening morale and supporting the military campaign in Yemen
   c. aggressively reacting to interference in U.S. elections and cyberattacks

C Translate the following Japanese into English. Then listen to the CD and practice the conversation with your partner.　　　◎ CD 15

A: Hey, did you catch the president's speech last night?
B: You bet I did. ¹· _____

_____.

A: I'm sure our colleagues all feel the same way.
B: Of course. ²· _____

_____.

A: What would you expect, when former President Trump shrank the diplomatic corps?
B: ³· Well,_____

_____.

A: His words were welcome, but let's see if he can keep his promises.

1. 私たちを応援していると言ってくれて，とても安心しました。

2. この４年間，国務省職員の士気は非常に低かったのです。

3. まあ，バイデン大統領の政策は，トランプ大統領とはかなり違うようです。

D Summary Practice: Fill in the blanks with suitable words beginning with the letters indicated.　　　　　　　　　　　　　　　　　◎ CD 16

In his first big (¹· **f**　　　　　　) (²· **p**　　　　　) speech, President Joseph Biden spelled out the direction he plans for the U.S., summing it up in three words: America is (³· **b**　　　). Biden's focus on rebuilding (⁴· **a**　　　　　) with America's (⁵· **a**　　　) is a sharp (⁶· **d**　　　　　　) from the policies adopted during (⁷· **T**　　　　　　) presidency. With a promise to lead with (⁸· **d**　　　　　), Biden declared that the (⁹· **S**　　　) (¹⁰· **D**　　　　　　), shrunk in (¹¹· **s**　　) and (¹²· **i**　　　　　　) during the Trump years, would be at the (¹³· **h**　　　) of his new policy. From the (¹⁴· **c**　　) on the number of (¹⁵· **r**　　　　　) allowed into the U.S. to the military (¹⁶· **c**　　　　　) in (¹⁷· **Y**　　　　), Biden's vision appears to be broad. He also had (¹⁸· **s**　　　) words for America's (¹⁹· **a**　　　　　), Russia, citing its interference in U.S. (²⁰· **e**　　　　), cyberattacks and (²¹· **p**　　　　) its own citizens. Time will tell if the new president will be able to (²²· **f**　　　) his promises.

E Discussion: Share your ideas and opinions with your classmates.

1. How much do you know about President Biden? See what you can find out about his family background and the policies he campaigned on. In what ways did his family background influence his policies?

2. Several differences between President Biden and former President Trump are mentioned in this news story. Choose one of the issues below and see if you can find information about the two presidents' policy differences.

　　　　　　the environment　　　gay rights　　　women's issues

3. Look for updated information on the major accomplishments of the Biden administration so far. Do you think America is "back"?

Coast-to-Coast Storms

Air Date: January 26 2021
Duration: 2′ 05″

Preview Questions

1. What types of severe weather are being experienced in the U.S.?
——アメリカではどのような厳しい天候に見舞われていますか。

2. What is the extent of the damage?
——被害はどの程度まで及んでいますか。

Warm-up Exercises

A Vocabulary Check: Choose the correct definition for each of the words below.

1. treacherous ( )
2. pierce ( )
3. massive ( )
4. sustain ( )
5. debris ( )

a. huge; extremely large
b. scattered pieces of waste
c. to penetrate
d. to endure
e. dangerous; unsafe

B **Fill in the blanks with appropriate expressions from the Vocabulary Check above. Change the word forms where necessary.**

1. The bomb left the area littered with (   ).
2. His car was totaled, but Ted only (   ) a few bruises. He was lucky.
3. When rays of sunshine finally (   ) through the dark clouds, we decided to go for a swim.
4. A (   ) rock was blocking the mountain road, so we were forced to turn back.
5. How can you think of driving in this snow storm? The icy roads will be (   ).

News Story [2' 05"]

D. Muir: We're also tracking several storms on the move at this hour. Alerts in at least 25 states tonight. And we have now learned that deadly tornado in Fultondale, Alabama was at least an EF-2. Winds of up to 135 miles per hour.

5

A teenager killed while hiding in the basement with his family. Tonight, the story of another family surviving, sheltering in a bathtub. Marcus Moore now from Alabama.

10

M. Moore: Tonight, ¹· _____
making travel treacherous for millions. Up to a foot of blowing snow in spots, and ice. In Michigan, a police dash cam capturing a car sliding off the road. In the Deep South, tornado sirens piercing the night as the storm closed in on communities north and east of Birmingham.

15

J. Spann, meteorologist: So, if you are in that polygon, ²· _____
_____.

M. Moore: First responders launching a massive search and rescue operation. This hotel ripped apart. Terrified guests inside.

N. Martin, tornado survivor: The lights were gone. The internal sirens were going off. 3. _____ _____.

M. Moore: Daylight revealing a town torn to pieces. Meteorologists believe it was at least a high-end EF-2 tornado with 135-mile-per-hour winds. Some 30 people hurt. Tragically, a 14-year-old boy sheltering in a basement with his family did not survive.

We met Brittany Vice who rode out the storm with her two-month-old daughter, Hallie, 4. _____ _____.

B. Vice: Got them up, went to the bathroom and the dogs didn't even make it to the door before the tornado hit.

M. Moore: So it was that quick?

B. Vice: It was that quick.

M. Moore: Just down the street, Michael Holloway 5. _____ _____.

M. Holloway: With me being as big of a guy as I am, I got into as small of a ball as I could and I prayed.

M. Moore: The severe weather one of several storms hitting the country this week. The separate system to blame for this pile-up on I-25 in Colorado. Six people were hurt.

David, we are back outside that hotel that sustained serious damage. There are cars here crushed under the heavy debris. And by all accounts, 6. _____ and those in its path had only minutes to take cover. David?

D. Muir: All part of that major system. We're thinking about those families. Marcus, thank you.

Notes   tracking「(進路を) 追跡している；監視している」 deadly tornado「死者が出るほどの (激しい) 竜巻」 Fultondale「フルトンデール〈アラバマ州北部に位置する都市〉」 EF-2「EF (スケール 2)〈= Enhanced Fujita scale; EF-Scale 被害の大きさなどから竜巻の強さを評定する尺度で，EF-0 ～ EF-5 までの 6 段階で竜巻の分類がなされている。EF-5 が最大〉」 in spots「所々で」 dash cam「ドライブレコーダー；ダッシュボード・カメラ；車載カメラ」 Birmingham「バーミングハム〈アラバマ州北部に位置する同州最大の都市〉」 polygon「(地図上に表示された注意喚起) 地域；多角形」 First responders「ファースト・レスポンダー；第一 (初期) 対応者〈災害や事故による負傷者に対して，救助隊・救急隊・消防隊・警察など最初に対応する人〉」 internal sirens「(危険を知らせる) ホテル内のサイレン (警報装置)」 going off「突然鳴りだす；突然作動する」 high-end「トップクラスの」 rode out ~「～を乗り切った；～を切り抜けた」 make it to ~「～までたどり着く」 got into as small of a ball as I could「(強風で飛ばされないように) できるだけ体を小さくしていた」 The severe weather … this week.「= The severe weather (was) one of several storms (that was) hitting the country this week.」 separate system「別の嵐」 I-25「州間高速道路 25 号線〈= Interstate 25 奇数番号は基本的に南北に走る高速道路〉」 by all accounts「みんなの話では；誰に聞いても」 take cover「避難する」

After   You Watch the News

Exercises

A Listen to the CD and fill in the blanks in the text.   CD 17

B Mark the following sentences true (T) or false (F) according to the information in the news story.

(   ) **1.** Thirty people were injured by the tornado, but there was no loss of life.

(   ) **2.** Sirens were used to warn people to get off the icy roads.

(   ) **3.** Some families sheltered in bathtubs and basements to try to survive the tornadoes.

(   ) **4.** Survivors of the tornado in Alabama include the hotel guests as well as Brittany Vice and her baby.

(   ) **5.** First responders began a search and rescue operation following the EF-2 tornado.

(   ) **6.** Most people survived the tornado because they had ample time to take cover.

C Translate the following Japanese into English. Then listen to the CD and practice the conversation with your partner. ⊙ CD 18

A: Brittany, thank goodness you are all okay!

B: It's really a miracle. ¹· _____

_____.

A: ²· _____?

B: Yes! ³· <u>When we heard the siren,</u>_____

_____. Everything happened so quickly.

A: Little Hallie must have been so scared.

B: We all were! But we survived.

A: That's something to be grateful for.

1. 私たちの町全体がずたずたに破壊されてしまいました。
2. バスタブの中で嵐を乗り切ったというのは本当ですか。
3. サイレンを聞いたとき，数分で避難しなければならないことがわかりました。

D Summary Practice: Fill in the blanks with suitable words beginning with the letters indicated. ⊙ CD 19

Americans all across the (¹· **c**   ) have been experiencing
(²· **s**   ) weather that has resulted in the (³· **m**   )
destruction of buildings, with one teenager (⁴· **k**   ). The
(⁵· **w**   ) storms are so widespread that there are currently
(⁶· **a**   ) out in at least (⁷· **t**   )-(⁸· **f**   ) states. A
tornado that struck Fultondale, (⁹· **A**   ) has been categorized
as at least an EF-2, with 135-mile-per-hour (¹⁰· **w**   ) that left cars
(¹¹· **c**   ) and a (¹²· **t**   ) torn to pieces. (¹³· **F**   )
(¹⁴· **r**   ) carrying out (¹⁵· **s**   ) and
(¹⁶· **r**   ) operations found (¹⁷· **t**   ) survivors in a
(¹⁸· **h**   ) that had been ripped apart. Local families sheltered in their
(¹⁹· **b**   ) and basements, some (²⁰· **p**   ) that
they would survive the (²¹· **d**   ) storm. And most of them did,
despite having only (²²· **m**   ) to find shelter. Sadly, one
(²³· **t**   ) lost his life.

E **Discussion: Share your ideas and opinions with your classmates.**

1. Several types of severe weather are mentioned in this news story. What are they? Do any of them occur in your area? How many have you experienced?

2. Look online and see what you can find out about tornadoes. How are they different from typhoons and hurricanes?

3. Choose one of the American states mentioned in the news report. Do an internet search to see what you can learn. Share your findings with the class.

Hank Aaron: Baseball Legend

Sipa USA/Jiji Press Photo

Before You Watch the News

Air Date: January 22 2021
Duration: 2′ 45″

Preview Questions

1. Why was Hank Aaron referred to as a baseball legend?
　　——ハンク・アーロンはなぜ野球界のレジェンドと呼ばれていたのですか。

2. Besides baseball, what else was he known for?
　　——野球の他，彼は何で有名でしたか。

Warm-up Exercises

A Vocabulary Check: Choose the correct definition for each of the words below.

1. slug （　　）   **a.** a huge number of

2. legendary （　　）   **b.** to hit hard; to whack

3. heckle （　　）   **c.** firm; resolute

4. unshakeable （　　）   **d.** to express disapproval in a loud voice

5. zillions of （　　）   **e.** renowned; celebrated

B **Fill in the blanks with appropriate expressions from the Vocabulary Check above. Change the word forms where necessary.**

1. Are you joking? Our budget is way too small to invite that (   ) jazz singer to our event.

2. Pat's nice, but she always asks (   ) personal questions.

3. The politician was (   ) by the crowd when he suggested raising taxes.

4. Did you hear about Jim? He had too much to drink and (   ) Jake!

5. Mark is (   ). He'll never move back to New York.

News Story [2′ 45″]

D. Muir: And tonight, across this country, the nation celebrating the life of Hall of Famer Hank Aaron. A rare legend among legends. He became baseball's home run king, the first to break Babe Ruth's record. A champion of civil rights on and off the field. Here's Steve Osunsami.

5

S. Osunsami: [1.] _____ for this mighty swing…

10

Announcer: Straightaway. Fastball. It's a high drive into deep left center field. Buckner goes back to the fence. It is gone!

S. Osunsami: …that helped replace a white man with a black man in the record books. This was the call that night in Georgia in 1974 when Hank Aaron slugged his way past the legendary Babe Ruth with 715 career home runs, and his record of 755 would [2.] _____ _____.

15

Announcer: A black man is getting a standing ovation in the Deep South for breaking a record of an all-time baseball idol.

S. Osunsami: But it needs to be said that Hank Aaron overcame a whole lot

20

more than a baseball record. He was heckled by racist white fans and players. **3.** _____ _____ to kidnap his children, and the death threats came pouring in the mail.

H. Aaron: I couldn't open a letter for… for… for months. They had to be opened by the FBI or somebody else, you know. I couldn't let that stand in my way.

S. Osunsami: Henry Louis Aaron grew up poor in Alabama, where he had to make his own baseball bats with tree limbs. It was when black athletes were lucky if they could make it to the Negro Leagues, which were separate and certainly **4.** _____.

H. Aaron: I played with some ball players that knew how to play the game, and they taught me an awful lot.

S. Osunsami: Mr. Aaron was unshakeable, living up to the great responsibility he felt for how he represented black Americans. **5.** _____ _____, gave millions to schools and charities, and just weeks ago was part of an effort encouraging black Americans to get vaccinated for the coronavirus.

H. Aaron: It's just a small thing that can help zillions of people in this country.

S. Osunsami: **6.** _____, he would often say that he wanted to be remembered most for the lives he helped change.

H. Aaron: I think that I wanna be remembered as someone who was able to forget about baseball, but be able to… to… help mankind.

S. Osunsami: The Atlanta stadium where Hank Aaron made history is long gone. It was torn down years ago and this parking lot is what's left. But they've kept a piece of the outfield wall **7.** _____ _____. Hank Aaron was 86 years old and the Atlanta Braves tells us tonight that he died peacefully in his sleep.

Notes **Hall of Famer**「殿堂入りした人」 **champion of civil rights**「公民権の擁護者」 **on and off the field**「フィールドの内外を問わず」 **Straightaway**「ストレート；直球」 **high drive**「(打球が) 高々と上がって」 **Buckner**「バックナー (外野手)〈William Joseph Buckner: 1960〜1990 年代にアメリカメジャー・リーグで活躍した外野手。ハンク・アーロンの打ったホームランボールを追って外野フェンスをよじ登った 1974 年には，ロサンゼルス・ドジャーズでプレイしていた〉」 **all-time**「これまで (野球史上) 最高の」 **I couldn't let that stand in my way**「それが原因で，自分のやるべきこと (やりたいこと) を邪魔されたくありませんでした」 **make it to ~**「〜までたどり着く」 **living up to ~**「(責任など) を背負って (生きる)；(期待など) に沿って・応えて (生活する)」

Background of the News

　メジャーリーグ (MLB: Major League Baseball) で歴代2位の 755 本塁打の記録を持つハンク・アーロンさんが 86 歳で，2021 年 1 月 22 日に死去した。1976 年に引退するまでに放った，通算 755 本塁打は 2007 年にバリー・ボンズに抜かれるまでメジャーリーグ記録だった。また，通算 2297 打点は歴代最多で，1982 年には米野球殿堂 (Hall of Fame) 入りを果たしている。

　アーロンさんは，黒人が MLB でプレーすることを禁止されていた時代に，人種隔離政策が敷かれていたアメリカ南部に生まれた。1974 年，白人の大打者ベーブ・ルースの持つ通算 714 号の記録更新に迫り始めると，人種差別者 (racist) からは「これ以上打つな」という脅迫が相次ぎ，自宅には家族の生命を脅かすような手紙さえも届いたという。

　現役を退いた後，アーロンさんは MLB でフロント入りした初の黒人幹部の 1 人になり，アトランタ・ブレーブスで働いた。また，公民権団体として有名な「全米黒人地位向上協会」(NAACP: National Association for the Advancement of Colored People) の慈善活動部門で幹部として貢献した。

After | You Watch the News

Exercises

A Listen to the CD and fill in the blanks in the text.　　　　　 CD 20

B Multiple Choice Questions

1. Which of the following statements is *NOT* mentioned in the news story as describing Hank Aaron?

　a. He was heckled by white fans for playing in the Negro League.

　b. He was a legendary baseball player and a successful businessman.

　c. He was poor when he was young but later gave away millions of dollars.

2. Hank Aaron broke Babe Ruth's record when

    a. he hit his 715th home run.

    b. he entered the Baseball Hall of Fame.

    c. he held his home run record for 30 years.

3. Hank Aaron mostly wanted to be remembered

    a. for breaking Babe Ruth's record.

    b. for forgetting about baseball and helping others.

    c. for becoming a baseball legend in spite of death threats.

4. Hank Aaron

    a. received death threats because he was a champion for civil rights.

    b. was proud of earning millions of dollars as a businessman.

    c. made history at a ballpark in Atlanta that is now the site of a parking lot.

C **Translate the following Japanese into English. Then listen to the CD and practice the conversation with your partner.**   ⊙ CD 21

A: Dad, when we go to Atlanta next month, do you think we can catch a Braves game?

B: I don't see why not. But why the sudden interest in the Braves?

A: Well, my teacher was talking about Hank Aaron today. ¹· She said _____

_____.

B: That he was. He broke Babe Ruth's record. I remember that game!

A: Yeah—and he got a standing ovation. I want to see the stadium where that happened.

B: ²· _____ but we

can see a piece of the wall.

A: Let's go! ³· Our teacher also said _____

_____. He's my new hero.

1. 先生は，彼が野球のホームラン王と呼ばれていたと言っていたよ。

2. そのスタジアムはもうだいぶ前になくなっているけれど，壁の一部を見ることができるよ。

3. 私たちの先生も，彼は多くの人々を様々な方法で助けたと言っていたよ。

D **Summary Practice: Fill in the blanks with suitable words beginning with the letters indicated.** ⊙ CD 22

Baseball legend Hank Aaron has died peacefully in his sleep at the age of (¹· **e**   )-(²· **s**   ). Known for his (³· **m**   ) swing, Aaron was perhaps best known for breaking the home run (⁴· **r**   ) of baseball idol (⁵· **B**   ) (⁶· **R**   ) back in 1974—a time when most black athletes were in the (⁷· **N**   ) (⁸· **L**   ) if they played at all. That record-breaking hit got Aaron a standing (⁹· **o**   ) as well as heckling and (¹⁰· **d**   ) (¹¹· **t**   ) from (¹²· **r**   ) athletes and fans.

As a boy in (¹³· **A**   ), Aaron was so poor that he had to make his own baseball bats out of tree (¹⁴· **l**   ). In spite of his many challenges, he had a strong sense of (¹⁵· **r**   ) about his role in representing (¹⁶· **b**   ) Americans. He wanted to be (¹⁷· **r**   ) for the way he helped change the lives of others— and that he did, through his generous donations to schools and (¹⁸· **c**   ). One of the last things he did was to encourage black Americans to get a (¹⁹· **c**   ) vaccination. During his life, Aaron championed civil (²⁰· **r**   ) both on and off the baseball field.

E **Discussion: Share your ideas and opinions with your classmates.**

1. Who are some other baseball legends? Select one of them and do an internet search to see what you can learn. Share your finding with the class.

2. According to this news story, Hank Aaron wanted to be remembered for helping people. Think of other athletes who had a personal impact on other people. In what ways did they help them?

3. What is your favorite sport to play? To watch? If you could try a new sport, which one would you choose? Explain your reasons.

News Story 8

Turtles Rescued from the Cold

Before You Watch the News

Air Date: February 25 2021
Duration: 1' 34"

Preview Questions

1. What happened to the sea turtles in Texas?
——テキサスのウミガメに何が起こりましたか。

2. How are they being helped?
——ウミガメはどのようにして助けられているのですか。

Warm-up Exercises

A Vocabulary Check: Choose the correct definition for each of the words below.

1. brutal ( )
2. flipper ( )
3. instinct ( )
4. tub ( )
5. underway ( )

a. a deep, round container
b. severe; harsh
c. an inborn pattern of behavior in animals
d. in progress; continuing
e. the limb of a sea animal used for swimming

B Fill in the blanks with appropriate expressions from the Vocabulary Check above. Change the word forms where necessary.

1. We reported to the staff that the seal's right (   ) seemed to be injured.
2. Look for a plastic (   ) for the goldfish until we can buy a proper tank.
3. Construction of the new building should be (   ) by summer.
4. Dozens of people had to be hospitalized due to the (   ) heat.
5. Those birds have an (   ) to fly south in the winter.

News Story [1′ 34″]

D. Muir: Finally tonight here, the volunteers saving the sea turtles. Definitely "America Strong."

Tonight, the remarkable images, saving the sea turtles in Texas. They've been at it for days.

5

Volunteer: Off you go, turtle buds.

D. Muir: The sea turtles had been rescued from the brutal cold. **1.** _____
_____.

Scientists tell us the sea turtles that survived recovered after what's   10
called a cold stun to their system.

W. Knight, Executive Director, Sea Turtle, Inc.: They can't move their flippers, so they float to the top of the water. And even though their instinct tells them **2.** _____, they can't.

D. Muir: Volunteers first saving them from the ocean during the storms, trying   15
to keep them warm enough. The group Sea Turtle, Inc. among the groups helping. Small tubs to keep them warm. And all this week, **3.** _____
_____. The University of Texas Marine Science Institute, too.

J. Tunnell, Reserve Director, Univ. of Texas Marine Science Institute: 20

Hey, David.

D. Muir: Reserve Director, Jace Tunnell.

J. Tunnell: We actually had 900 sea turtles that we, that came into the center. Look here, *4.* _____

_____

_____ that we kept behind, so that we're able to give them a little more treatment.

D. Muir: Tonight, Jace and the team releasing 870 turtles and counting. In Corpus Christi, the Texas State Aquarium with U-Hauls full of rescued turtles, warming them in tanks.

J. Gilbert, Sr. Vice President & COO, Texas State Aquarium: Hi, David.

D. Muir: Jesse Gilbert with the aquarium, tonight, telling us those turtles are going home.

J. Gilbert: Happy to report that we're able to release 950 turtles back into the Gulf of Mexico.

D. Muir: The sea turtles saved tonight, *5.* _____

_____.

We needed some good news. A remarkable effort, underway for days now. I'm David Muir. I'll see you tomorrow. Good night.

Notes   **They've been at it**「作業を続けている」 **turtle buds**「カメさんたち〈buds は buddies の省略形〉」 **cold stun**「コールドスタン〈低下した水温に一定期間いることでショック状態に陥ったり,体の機能が低下したりする状態のことで,死に至ることもある〉」 **system**「(人や動物の)体」 **Executive Director**「代表;事務局長」 **Sea Turtle, Inc.**「シータートル・インク〈ウミガメの保護団体〉」 **The University of Texas Marine Science Institute**「テキサス大学海洋科学研究所」 **Reserve Director**「リザーブディレクター;保護担当所長」 **Corpus Christi**「コーパスクリスティ〈テキサス州南部の港市で,コーパスクリスティ湾に位置する〉」 **Texas State Aquarium**「テキサス州立水族館」 **U-Hauls**「ユーホール〈アメリカの U-Haul 社の引っ越し用レンタルトレーラー・トラック〉」 **Sr. Vice President & COO**「上級副社長兼 COO〈COO = chief operating officer;最高(業務)執行責任者〉」 **the Gulf of Mexico**「メキシコ湾」

After You Watch the News

Exercises

A Listen to the CD and fill in the blanks in the text. CD 23

B Multiple Choice Questions

1. What are the volunteers doing to the sea turtles before releasing them?
   a. rescuing and warming them
   b. giving them a cold stun and then rescuing them
   c. saving them from the ocean and giving them a bath

2. As a result of the cold stun, many sea turtles
   a. use their flippers to move to warmer water.
   b. are unable to move their flippers or lift their heads.
   c. are only able to do what their instinct tells them to do.

3. The Marine Science Institute
   a. is hoping to keep some of the sea turtles to put on display.
   b. has released all of the injured sea turtles into the Gulf of Mexico.
   c. is keeping some turtles longer than others to give them extra care.

4. The effort to save the sea turtles
   a. has involved many volunteers over several days.
   b. has been successfully completed thanks to the volunteers.
   c. involved exactly the same kind of treatment for every sea turtle.

C Translate the following Japanese into English. Then listen to the CD and practice the conversation with your partner.　　　　　◎ CD 24

A: Did you see those sea turtles on TV last night?

B: On television? What did they do?

A: ¹·During the recent storms, _____

_____ .

B: That's terrible! Did they all die?

A: No. ²· _____

_____ .

B: What happens after they are warmed up?

A: ³· _____ .

Remarkable, isn't it?

1. 最近の暴風雨で，彼らの体は猛烈な寒さのためにコールドスタンを起こしたのです。
2. 大規模なボランティアチームが彼らを救出し，たらいやタンクで暖めました。
3. カメは海に戻されます。

D Summary Practice: Fill in the blanks with suitable words beginning with the letters indicated.　　　　　◎ CD 25

A team of (¹· v　　　　　　　) in (²· T　　　　　) is credited with saving the lives of hundreds of sea turtles who were exposed to brutally (³· c　　　) temperatures during the recent (⁴· s　　　　　). While (⁵· i　　　　　　) tells the turtles to move their (⁶· f　　　　　) and lift their heads to (⁷· b　　　　　), they were unable to do so as a result of so-called cold (⁸· s　　　). Volunteers from (⁹· S　　　) (¹⁰· T　　　　　　), Inc. and the (¹¹· M　　　　　) Science (¹²· I　　　　　), who rescued the creatures from the (¹³· o　　　　), knew that their bodies had to be (¹⁴· w　　　　　). The Texas (¹⁵· S　　　) (¹⁶· A　　　　　　) got involved as well, with U-Hauls full of (¹⁷· t　　　　) in which to warm the turtles. So far, (¹⁸· e　　　) hundred (¹⁹· s　　　　　) of the animals have been (²⁰· r　　　　　) by the Marine Science Institute, while the Texas State Aquarium reports it is releasing 950 of the animals back into the Gulf of Mexico. Now that's a happy ending!

E Discussion: Share your ideas and opinions with your classmates.

1. How much do you know about sea turtles? Do a search to see what you can learn about these fascinating marine animals. Share your findings with the class.

2. Three organizations mentioned in the news story are Sea Turtle, Inc., the University of Texas Marine Science Institute and the Texas State Aquarium. Select one of them and do an internet search to learn about their activities.

3. No mention is made in the news story about why the "cold stun" occurred. Brainstorm possible reasons with your classmates.

　英語では子音が連続して現れることが多いが，日本人はどうしても子音と子音の間に不必要な母音を入れて発音しがちである。例えば turtle /tɚːtl/ では /t/ と /l/ とが連続してきている。これを「タートル」と，いわゆるカタカナ読みをしてしまえば，本来の英語の発音にはならない。余分な母音が入らないようにするためには，/t/ で舌先を歯茎につけ，舌先をつけたまま，/l/ に移行して呼気を勢いよく舌の横から抜くように発音するとよい。「トル（トゥル）」より「トー（トォ）」に近い音になる。

— Finally tonight here, the volunteers saving the sea *turtles*.

(Turtles Rescued from the Cold, p.45)

— The sea *turtles* had been rescued from the *brutal* cold.

(Turtles Rescued from the Cold, p.45)

　語尾が "-le(-al)" で，その前に子音が来るときにもこの発音になる。"couple" は，「カップル」のように，語尾発音が /-pulu/ とならないにように注意が必要である。

— Ah… we did a *couple* of Zoom calls with Archie.

(Queen: Family Saddened, p.73)

— We were going a *little* stir-crazy on lockdown.　　*(Easter Egg Hunt, p.2)*

— But every *little* bit kind of helps and every *little* bit, …

(Easter Egg Hunt, p.3)

— …, so that we're able to give them a *little* more treatment.

(Turtles Rescued from the Cold, p.46)

News Story 9

Suez Canal Bottleneck

Air Date: March 28 2021
Duration: 1' 29"

Preview Questions

1. What is happening in the Suez Canal?

——スエズ運河で何が起きていますか。

2. How might that affect people in the U.S.?

——それはアメリカの人々にどのような影響を与えそうですか。

Warm-up Exercises

A **Vocabulary Check: Choose the correct definition for each of the words below.**

1. resume (　　)

2. dislodge (　　)

3. vital (　　)

4. stranded (　　)

5. harsh (　　)

a. severe

b. run aground; stuck

c. to restart; to begin again

d. to move or force out of a tight position

e. absolutely necessary; essential

B Fill in the blanks with appropriate expressions from the Vocabulary Check above. Change the word forms where necessary.

1. Good team spirit is (   ) if we want to win the match.
2. Unable to tolerate the (   ) winter weather, Ken moved back south after just one year in the north.
3. Dozens of tourists photographed the (   ) whale on the beach.
4. Are you excited for classes to (   ) after the summer break?
5. We had to (   ) several large rocks in order to get into the cave.

News Story [1′ 29″]

L. Davis: Efforts to try to refloat that massive ship blocking the Suez Canal are expected to resume tomorrow. This new video shows dredgers moving tons of sand, hoping to dislodge the Ever Given,

1. _____

_____. More than 300 ships waiting nearby unable to get through the waterway. The economic impact could soon be felt here at home. Here's ABC's Deirdre Bolton.

D. Bolton: Tonight, this major traffic jam caused by that megaship stuck

2. _____, potentially affecting wallets here at home. Around 12% of global trade goes through the Suez Canal, a vital shipping artery. Coffee, furniture, car parts, all trapped on more than 300 stranded ships, costing industries nearly $10 billion a day in container cargo alone. Costs likely to be passed on to consumers.

P. De Haas, head of Petroleum Analysis, Gasbuddy: The fact that, uh, now we're seeing a backlog, it could have ripple effects here in the U.S.

D. Bolton: The blockage is also affecting 10% of the global crude oil supply.

3. _____ had been moving higher

in the U.S., due in part to the
harsh winter in Texas that hurt
production.

P. De Haas: At some point this summer,
we could see a national average of
$3 a gallon.

5

D. Bolton: Tonight, the Murphy family wondering if they'll be able to afford
4. _____.

B. Murphy, motorist: If the prices keep going up, we're going to have to cancel
our plans.

10

D. Bolton: The national average for a gallon of gasoline, at $2.86. That is
already 70% higher than where we were 5. _____
_____. And we are still weeks away from the peak travel
season.

Notes　**dredgers**「浚渫（しゅんせつ）船〈運河などの底面にたまった土砂などを取り去る土木工事を行う船〉」
the Ever Given「（大型コンテナ船）エバーギブン」　**megaship**「巨大船」　**wallets**「財布（経済）」
shipping artery「（重要な）幹線航路」　**container cargo**「コンテナ貨物」　**passed on to ~**「~に
転嫁される」　**head of Petroleum Analysis, Gasbuddy**「ガスバディ社石油分析部長〈ガスバディ
社は，地域で最も安価なガソリンスタンドを見つけられるように支援するアプリやウェブサイトを運営
するハイテク企業〉」　**backlog**「バックログ；（仕事や注文などの）未処理分；未処理案件；残務〈日
を追うごとに待機中の貨物運搬船が多くなっている状態〉」　**ripple effects**「連鎖反応」

Background of the News

スエズ運河（the Suez Canal）は 1869 年に開通し，英仏の支配をへて，エジプトが 1956 年に国有化を宣言した。アジアと欧州を最短距離で結ぶこの運河は，総延長約 193 キロメートルで，世界の海上輸送物資の約 12％が通る大動脈として物流を支えている。自動車や家電製品，医薬品など単価の高い商品を運ぶ船舶が年間 2 万隻近く利用しているという。2021 年 3 月 27 日付の『毎日新聞』によれば，その通過料は 2020 年に 56 億ドル（約 6,112 億円）に上り，エジプトにとって大きな外貨獲得源になっている。

今回，コンテナ船「エバーギブン」号（the Ever Given）は，中国からオランダへ貨物を運ぶ途中，2021 年 3 月 23 日にスエズ運河で座礁した。全長約 400 メートルの巨大船（megaship）は強風にあおられて航路を外れ，船首部分が運河のへりに衝突し，幅約 300 メートルの水路（waterway）を塞いだ。エジプト運河当局は事故を受け，運河への船舶の進入を停止したが，運河には既にコンテナ船や石油タンカー，穀物運搬船など約 400 隻が足止めされた（stranded）。浚渫（しゅんせつ）船（dredger）による作業の末，船は同 29 日に離礁（dislodge）に成功したものの，世界の物流に大きな影響が出た。

この大型コンテナ船は，愛媛県今治市に本社がある日本の海運会社所有の船舶で，台湾の海運会社が運航していた。エジプト運河庁は，作業にかかった費用のほか，運河閉鎖に伴う通航料収入の損失への賠償として，5 億 5 千万ドル（約 600 億円）を請求していた。今治市の汽船会社側とスエズ運河庁側の賠償金をめぐる訴訟は 2021 年 7 月 7 日に和解した。賠償金の合意額は公表されていないものの，船主が加入している保険で賄われるとされている。

After | You Watch the News

Exercises

A Listen to the CD and fill in the blanks in the text.　　　　⊙ CD 26

B Multiple Choice Questions

1. The Ever Given
   a. is carrying $10 billion of container cargo.
   b. will hopefully be dislodged within six days.
   c. is holding up global trade because it is stuck.

2. Which statement describes what is currently taking place in the Suez Canal?

    a. There is a 6,000-mile traffic jam of cargo-carrying ships.

    b. One megaship is blocking the passage of more than 300 ships.

    c. Twelve percent of global trade has been stopped due to harsh weather.

3. Which of the following is *NOT* a likely consequence of the Suez Canal incident?

    a. higher prices of coffee and car parts in the U.S.

    b. an increase in the number of megaships allowed to use the Canal

    c. the amount of money industries will have to pay for container cargo

4. The price of gasoline in the U.S.

    a. is over 50% higher than at this time last year.

    b. is currently at a national average of $3 a gallon.

    c. reached a high of $2.86 a gallon in the peak travel season.

C **Translate the following Japanese into English. Then listen to the CD and practice the conversation with your partner.**   ◎ CD 27

A: 1. _____
_____?

B: Well, it's not looking good. I paid $2.90 a gallon for gas yesterday.

A: Wow! Don't you think gas might get cheaper as we head into summer?

B: No, it's just the opposite. 2. _____
_____.

A: But we promised the kids we'd take them to Disneyland in August, remember?

B: 3. _____.
Driving all the way to California is out of the question.

A: They'll be so disappointed! Well, I guess we'll have to plan another camping trip.

1. この夏，予定していたドライブ旅行ができると思いますか。

2. 旅行シーズンのピーク時にはガソリン価格は上昇します。

3. その頃にはガソリンが１ガロン３ドルになっている可能性が高いのです。

D Summary Practice: Fill in the blanks with suitable words beginning with the letters indicated.

CD 28

It is now day six of the major (¹· t   ) (²· j   ) in the (³· S   )
(⁴· C   ) with the megaship Ever Given still stuck, blocking the way
for more than (⁵· t   ) (⁶· h   ) other ships to pass
through the major (⁷· w   ). Efforts to (⁸· d   )
the (⁹· m   ) ship will (¹⁰· r   ) tomorrow, but it might
be too late to stop it from affecting prices thousands of miles away. With
(¹¹· t   ) percent of (¹²· g   ) trade passing through this
vital shipping (¹³· a   ), items like (¹⁴· c   ) and
(¹⁵· f   ) carried by the (¹⁶· s   ) ships cost
industries almost $10 billion a day—costs which may eventually be passed
on to (¹⁷· c   ). The (¹⁸· r   ) effects could also
apply to oil and (¹⁹· g   ), with many Americans worried that the
already high gas prices might rise to a (²⁰· n   )
(²¹· a   ) of three dollars a gallon. The (²²· e   )
impact of the blocked waterway could be nasty.

E Discussion: Share your ideas and opinions with your classmates.

1. How much do you know about the Suez Canal? Where is it? When did it
become an important international waterway? Do an internet search to
learn more about the Canal. Share your findings with the class.

2. The news story mentions that coffee, furniture, car parts and crude oil
are among the many products that pass through the Suez Canal to be
traded globally. Do goods shipped to Japan pass through this major
waterway? See what you can learn about Japan's connection to the Canal.

Useful Grammar from the News　　③ 画像の説明は現在時制

　学習者にとって，テレビニュース英語の理解を助けてくれるのが，画像情報である。一般的に，音声のみでニュースを聞くより画像を見ながらの方が分かりやすい。ニュースキャスターが，現在（進行）形を用いて，画像とシンクロしながらニュースの説明をしてくれるからである。また，現在形を用いることで臨場感が生まれる。

— ***This new video shows*** dredgers moving tons of sand, hoping to dislodge the Ever Given, ...　　　　　　　　　*(Suez Canal Bottleneck, p.52)*

　上の例では，作業船が何トンもの砂を掘り出し，スエズ運河で立ち往生している巨大コンテナ船のエバーギブン号を動かそうとしている様子が映像として示されている。

— In a country devastated by war and terror, ***the Pope is here***, on a pilgrimage of peace.　　　　　　　　　　　*(Pope's Historic Trip, p.22)*

　「戦争とテロで荒廃したこの国で，ローマ教皇は平和巡礼の旅を続けています。」と，リポーターが教皇のイラク訪問を興奮気味に伝えている。大規模な野外ミサのためにスポーツ競技場に集まった熱狂的な信者たちが背景に映し出されている。視覚に訴えるこのような情報は，英語の聞き取りも助けてくれる。

— The Atlanta stadium where Hank Aaron made history is long gone. It was torn down years ago and ***this parking lot is*** what's left.
　　　　　　　　　　　　　　　　　　　　(Hank Aaron: Baseball Legend, p.40)

　ハンク・アーロンさんが以前に活躍したアトランタの球場は，すでに取り壊されているものの，駐車場は残っていると，リポーターがその駐車場から報告している。

First Female Eagle Scouts

Before You Watch the News

Air Date: February 21 2021
Duration: 1' 49"

Preview Questions

1. What are some young American women feeling proud of?
——アメリカの若い女性たちが誇りに思っていることは何ですか。

2. How did they achieve this goal?
——彼女らはどのようにしてこの目標を達成しましたか。

Warm-up Exercises

A Vocabulary Check: Choose the correct definition for each of the words below.

1. milestone ( )

2. soar ( )

3. inaugural ( )

4. adversity ( )

5. collectively ( )

a. difficulty; hardship

b. very important event; major achievement

c. as a group; as a whole

d. to take off; to rise quickly

e. first; marking the beginning of something

B Fill in the blanks with appropriate expressions from the Vocabulary
Check above. Change the word forms where necessary.

1. Students facing financial (   ) were advised to visit the office
   to learn about scholarships and loans.
2. The new debate team will be holding their (   ) event next
   Friday.
3. Today is such a special day! Graduation is a real (   ).
4. It was a huge project, but working (   ) the boys were able to
   complete the work on schedule.
5. Jeff delighted in seeing his model airplane (   ) into the air.

News Story [1′ 49″]

L. Davis: Finally tonight, "America
        Strong." The big virtual celebration
        in honor of some young ladies from
        across the country now emerging
        as pioneers.

5

Eagle Scout leader: I am proud to announce the first female class of Eagle
        Scouts.

L. Davis: In its 111-year history, this is a major milestone.

M. Torres: ¹· _____. I also wanted to
        prove to other girls that they could do it, too.

10

L. Davis: In 2019, the Boy Scouts of America became known as Scouts BSA.
        The name change, a game changer for girls like Sienna Eldert.

S. Eldert: You have to do so much work to get to where we are.

L. Davis: Where they are is in the history books. Nearly 1,000 young women
        ²· _____ soaring into the
        inaugural class of the first female Eagle Scouts. The accomplishment is
        so rare that, to date, only six percent of all scouts have achieved this
        status.

15

I. McQuiston: The fact that I can help lead and I can help recruit and I can show girls, like, in the face of adversity, you are strong, you are more than capable, and you are more than qualified. [3.] _____

_____

_____.

L. Davis: Collectively they've earned roughly 30,000 merit badges and provided an estimated 130,000 hours of community service [4.] _____ _____. For April Bowlin...

A. Bowlin: I had to do it, and I got through it.

L. Davis: ...reaching Eagle status, the highest rank in the organization, is a decades-old tradition in her family.

A. Bowlin: My grandpa and his brother. And then my stepdad and his three brothers and then my older brother.

L. Davis: Ming Torres can certainly relate.

M. Torres: I wanted to get it to prove to myself and to my family, like the boys in my family, that [5.] _____.

L. Davis: Girl power. Congratulations to that inaugural class taking their place in history. *GMA* first thing in the morning. David Muir is right back here tomorrow night. I'm Linsey Davis in New York. Good night.

Notes **Eagle Scouts**「イーグルスカウト〈ボーイスカウトの最高ランクで，優れたリーダーシップや協調性，コミュニティへの貢献などが求められる〉」 **the Boy Scouts of America**「ボーイスカウトアメリカ連盟；米国ボーイ・スカウト〈1910年に設立されたアメリカ最大規模の青少年運動組織〉」 **game changer**「ゲーム・チェンジャー；形勢を一変させる（考え方を根本から変える）出来事」 **merit badges**「メリット・バッジ；技能章〈応急手当て，キャンピングなど100以上もの技能分野において，能力が認められると付与されるバッジ〉」 **can certainly relate**「（イーグル・ステータスに到達したかったという状況や気持ちに）確かに共感できる」

After You Watch the News

Exercises

A Listen to the CD and fill in the blanks in the text. CD 29

B Multiple Choice Questions

1. The new Eagle Scouts

    a. are members of Scouts BSA.

    b. became part of the Boy Scouts of America in 2019.

    c. recently had a name change that was a game changer.

2. This group of female Eagle Scouts

    a. represents only six percent of all Scouts.

    b. is the first group of its kind in over 100 years.

    c. includes more than one thousand American women.

3. Which of the following does **NOT** describe how some of the new Eagle Scouts feel?

    a. determined to move up to the next rank

    b. proud that they have proved they can do what the boys do

    c. eager to inspire other girls by their achievements

4. April Bowlin

    a. performed 130,000 hours of community service.

    b. aimed to be better than the males in her family.

    c. followed in the footsteps of seven male family members.

C Translate the following Japanese into English. Then listen to the CD and practice the conversation with your partner.

◎CD 30

A: April just called me. She's an Eagle Scout!

B: 1. _____! That calls for a celebration.

A: It sure does. She said she had to do it, and she did it.

B: 2. _____
_____, you know.

A: I didn't realize that. Who else in the family has done it?

B: Her grandfather and her brother, and I think a bunch of other male relatives.

A: 3. And _____
_____. Girl power!

1. 実際，彼女はやり遂げたのです。
2. イーグル・スカウトになることは、彼女の家族にとって何十年もの伝統なのですよ。
3. そして，彼女は家族の中で女性として初めて最高位に就きました。

D Summary Practice: Fill in the blanks with suitable words beginning with the letters indicated.

◎CD 31

Tonight's "America Strong" focuses on a group of almost (¹· o____)
(²· t____) young women who are true (³· p____):
the (⁴· i____) group of female (⁵· E____) Scouts. The
celebration marks a (⁶· m____) in the 111-year
(⁷· h____) of the Scouting program. In fact, it was only in 2019 that
the name (⁸· B____) (⁹· S____) of America was changed to Scouts
(¹⁰· B____)—a (¹¹· g____) (¹²· c____) for strong young
(¹³· w____) like Sienna Eldert and April Bowlin. In spite of the
(¹⁴· p____), this group of young women (¹⁵· c____)
earned 30,000 (¹⁶· m____) (¹⁷· b____) and performed 130,000
hours of (¹⁸· c____) service, showing themselves and the
world that they are more than (¹⁹· q____).
(²⁰· C____) to these new Eagle Scouts for making
history!

E Discussion: Share your ideas and opinions with your classmates.

1. The Scouts are now an international youth organization. Do an internet search to find out more about their philosophy and their activities. Merit badges and community service are mentioned in the news story. See if you can learn more about them.

2. Many opportunities are opening up to create more challenges for girls and young women. Look for other examples and share them with the class. Are there similar examples in Japan?

Voting Law Backlash

Air Date: March 27 2021
Duration: 1' 31"

Before You Watch the News

Preview Questions

1. What recently happened with voting laws in the state of Georgia?
——ジョージア州の投票法において最近起きたことは何ですか。

2. What has been the reaction to these changes?
——この変更に対してどのような反響がありましたか。

Warm-up Exercises

A Vocabulary Check: Choose the correct definition for each of the words below.

1. sweeping (　　)　　**a.** a savage act; cruelty

2. atrocity (　　)　　**b.** obvious

3. punitive (　　)　　**c.** plans; strategy

4. tactics (　　)　　**d.** broad; extensive

5. blatant (　　)　　**e.** disciplinary; intended as punishment

B **Fill in the blanks with appropriate expressions from the Vocabulary Check above. Change the word forms where necessary.**

1. Joe's (   ) can be heavy-handed, but he gets results.

2. If you're caught speeding again, we will take (   ) actions.

3. Bill told you he broke up with Sally? That's a (   ) lie!

4. The new professor is noted for a book he wrote on war (   ).

5. The administration has promised to implement (   ) reforms.

News Story [1' 31"]

W. Johnson: Georgia's new voting law coming under fire. Critics calling it voter suppression, saying it unfairly targets voters of color. But supporters of the law, including the state's Republican governor

1. _____

_____, pushing back tonight. Here's ABC's Elizabeth Schulze.

E. Schulze: Tonight, protesters against that sweeping new election law taking to the streets in Georgia.

Protester: No justice.

Protesters: No peace.

E. Schulze: The law limits ballot drop boxes, tightens ID requirements for mail-in voting, and makes it a crime for anyone other than a poll worker to offer food and water to voters waiting in line. Critics say **2.** _____

_____.

President Biden calling it Jim Crow 2.0.

President J. Biden: It's an atrocity. This is nothing but punitive, designed to keep people from voting.

E. Schulze: But tonight, Georgia's Republican governor Brian Kemp pushing back.

Governor B. Kemp, Rep., Georgia: We're just gonna make sure it's a secure process and that those drop boxes are… are monitored.

E. Schulze: Kemp signing the bill behind closed doors, ^{3.} _____

_____.

Security guard: Quit. I said quit.

E. Schulze: While Democratic State Representative Park Cannon, a black woman, ^{4.} _____. Her lawyer speaking out to ABC News.

G. Griggs, attorney for Park Cannon: The rest of the country needs to take a very strong look at the tactics that are being used in Georgia.

E. Schulze: Now, dozens of other states with Republican-led legislatures are considering similar laws, ^{5.} _____

_____. Critics say it's a blatant attempt to suppress turnout in states that flipped for Democrats in the last election.

5

10

15

Notes   **under fire**「非難されている」 **pushing back**「反論している；押しのけている」 **taking to the streets**「(デモ隊が) 街に繰り出す」 **ballot drop boxes**「投票箱」 **mail-in voting**「郵便投票」 **Jim Crow 2.0**「ジム・クロウ 2.0；ジム・クロウ法の復活；新黒人差別 (政策)〈1870 年代以降，アメリカ南部諸州で定められた黒人に対する差別的法律の総称を Jim Crow Laws (ジム・クロウ法) と呼んだ〉」 **Democratic State Representative**「民主党の州議会議員」 **Republican-led legislatures**「共和党主導の議会」 **turnout**「投票者；投票率」 **flipped for ~**「～に鞍替えした；～支持に変更した」

Background of the News

アメリカ南部ジョージア州で，有権者の投票権を制限する内容を盛り込んだ選挙関連法が，共和党の主導で2021年3月25日に成立した。その内容は，郵便投票（mail-in voting）の本人確認に写真付きの身分証明書（ID）を義務付けるなど要件を厳格化し，投票行動を規制するものであった。

不在者投票での身分証明が厳しくなったが，黒人には運転免許証などの身分証明書を持たない人も多い。このため，ジョージア州人口の3割以上を占める黒人の投票を阻害するとして反発が強まっていた。

2021年5月10日付の『毎日新聞』によると，2020年の大統領選では黒人の87％，中南米系の61％がバイデン氏に投票しており，人種的少数派は民主党の支持基盤であることがうかがえる。この層は郵便・期日前投票の利用者も多かったという。

また，今回の法律には社会的に大きな反発も起きている。人権団体からは廃止を求めて提訴が相次ぎ，スポーツ界でも，メジャーリーグ（MLB：the Major League Baseball）が2021年7月のオールスターゲームをジョージア州のアトランタからコロラド州のデンバーに変更した。

After You Watch the News

Exercises

A Listen to the CD and fill in the blanks in the text.   CD 32

B Multiple Choice Questions

1. Which of the following statements is *NOT* mentioned about the new voting law in Georgia?

   a. It will probably make it more difficult for blacks to vote.

   b. It is supported by the state governor but not by the president.

   c. It is likely to increase the turnout of Republican voters in the state.

2. The new law includes

   a. stricter ID checks for people voting in person.

   b. a reduction in the number of ballot drop boxes.

   c. unlimited free water for people waiting in line to vote.

3. Who agrees with the protesters who have taken to the streets in Georgia?

    a. Brian Kemp

    b. Park Cannon

    c. both *a* and *b*

4. Which other states are considering similar laws?

    a. states that currently suppress voter turnout

    b. states with legislatures led by Republicans

    c. states where the presidential election process was not secure

C **Translate the following Japanese into English. Then listen to the CD and practice the conversation with your partner.**   **CD 33**

A: This new voting law is an absolute atrocity!

B: 1. _____.

A: 2. _____

    _____.

B: 3. _____

    _____. It's all garbage!

A: Yeah. And seeing all those white men surrounding him at the bill signing—and behind closed doors!

B: Talk about blatant racism.

A: The people of Georgia deserve better than this.

1. 大統領でさえジム・クロウ 2.0 と呼んでいます。

2. ケンプ知事はもっと広い視野を持っていると思っていました。

3. 彼はプロセスをしっかりさせるとか，投票箱を監視するとか言い続けています。

D Summary Practice: Fill in the blanks with suitable words beginning with the letters indicated.

CD 34

Georgia has a new (¹· **v**   ) law, and that new law has both
(²· **c**   ) and (³· **s**   ). Critics are claiming that
the law is (⁴· **p**   ), and will lead to voter (⁵· **s**   ).
Furthermore, they believe it unfairly (⁶· **t**   ) voters of
(⁷· **c**   ). Among the critics is the (⁸· **p**   ) himself, who
has called the law (⁹· **J**   ) (¹⁰· **C**   ) 2.0. Supporters like the Georgia
(¹¹· **g**   ), on the other hand, assert that voting in the state
will be a more (¹²· **s**   ) process when the law is enacted. Limiting
ballot (¹³· **d**   ) (¹⁴· **b**   ) and declaring it a (¹⁵· **c**   ) to
offer food and (¹⁶· **w**   ) to voters waiting in line seem outrageous to
people like Park Cannon, the (¹⁷· **D**   ) State
(¹⁸· **R**   ) who was arrested for trying to get into
the room where the bill was being signed into law. Her (¹⁹· **l**   )
warns that other states should look carefully at the (²⁰· **t**   ) being
used in Georgia.

E Discussion: Share your ideas and opinions with your classmates.

1. Do an internet search to find updated information on recent changes in the voting laws in the U.S.
2. Find a map showing which U.S. states are Democratic and which are Republican. Choose one state in each category and compare their voting laws. Share your findings with the class.
3. How does the voting process work in Japan? Who can vote? Is it possible to vote by mail or use ballot drop boxes? Are any concessions being made for elderly voters?

Queen: Family Saddened

AFP=JIJI

Air Date: March 9 2021
Duration: 3' 05"

Before You Watch the News

Preview Questions

1. What information about the royal family was revealed during Harry and Meghan's interview?
   ——ハリーとメーガンのインタビューによって，王室のどのような情報が明らかになりましたか。

2. What was the reaction of the Queen?
   ——女王の反応はどうでしたか。

Warm-up Exercises

A Vocabulary Check: Choose the correct definition for each of the words below.

1. explosive (　)
2. contemplate (　)
3. awkward (　)
4. dodge (　)
5. allegation (　)

a. accusation; claim that something wrong was done
b. uncomfortable; difficult
c. shocking; volatile
d. to avoid
e. to think carefully about

B **Fill in the blanks with appropriate expressions from the Vocabulary Check above. Change the word forms where necessary.**

1. The teacher urged the boys to (   ) their actions, hoping they would understand the severity of what they had done.

2. Jen felt (   ) when she met her fiance's former girlfriend.

3. The most exciting scene in the movie was when the superhero (   ) bullets to get to his plane.

4. After the third (   ) of sexual harassment, Fred was asked to leave his post.

5. In an (   ) new interview, the author admitted that he plagiarized parts of his latest bestseller.

News Story [3' 05"]

D. Muir: Overseas tonight, and Buckingham Palace is now responding after that interview with Harry and Meghan, including those accusations involving race. What the Queen is now saying tonight, and ABC's James Longman from London again, tonight.

5

J. Longman: Tonight, the Queen breaking [1.] _____ _____, responding to those explosive claims of racism 10 rocking the royal family. The new statement from Buckingham Palace saying, "The whole family is saddened to learn the full extent of how challenging the last few years have been for Harry and Meghan."

The response coming after Meghan revealed she contemplated suicide and accused an unnamed member of the royal family of racism, 15 [2.] _____ about how dark their baby's skin might be.

M. Markle, Duchess of Sussex: He won't be given security. He's not going to be given a title. And also, concerns and conversations about how dark his skin might be when he's born. 20

O. Winfrey, host: What?

J. Longman: Oprah asking Prince Harry about it, too.

O. Winfrey: What was that conversation?

Prince Harry, Duke of Sussex: That conversation, ^{3.} _____.
Ahm... but at the time, at the time, it was awkward. I was a bit shocked. Ahm...

O. Winfrey: Can you, can you tell us what the question was?

Prince Harry: No. I don't, I'm not comfortable with sharing that.

J. Longman: The Queen's statement didn't address those specific accusations, but said, "The issues raised, particularly that of race, are concerning." And added, "While some recollections may vary, they are taken very seriously and will be addressed by the family privately." Prince Harry told Oprah the comments were not made by the Queen or Prince Philip. Today, ^{4.} _____
since the interview aired in the UK...

Reporter: Sir, can I ask, what did you think of the interview?

J. Longman: ...Prince Charles dodged reporters. Sources say Prince Charles, the future king, believes diversity is Britain's greatest strength and is deeply concerned about the accusation.

R. Jobson, ABC News: Prince Harry has made extremely serious allegations, along with his wife, of racism, of systemic racism at the palace. You can't, then, say ^{5.} _____. It looks like they're sweeping it under the carpet.

J. Longman: Tonight, crisis talks reportedly underway at the palace. The Queen's three-sentence statement ending, "Harry, Meghan and Archie will always be much loved family members." And Harry and Meghan went out of their way to make it clear ^{6.} _____
_____.

Prince Harry: I've spoken more to my grandmother in the last year than I have done for many, many years.

O. Winfrey: Do you hold Zoom calls?

Prince Harry: Ah... we did a couple of Zoom calls with Archie.

M. Markle: Sometimes. Yeah, so they could see Archie. 5

O. Winfrey: Yeah?

Prince Harry: Ahm... my grandmother and I have a really good relationship and an understanding, and I have a deep respect for her. She's my colonel-in-chief. Right? Ahm... 7._____.

D. Muir: And, James, that was one of the interesting things about the Oprah 10 interview, that Harry and Meghan made it very clear, Harry's love for his grandmother and that they were still very much in touch with the Queen. These issues clearly much larger than their relationship with the Queen.

J. Longman: Yeah. They say 8._____ 15 _____ as a person, it's with the institution of the monarchy not responding to Meghan's pleas for help. But she still is, after all, the boss.

Notes accusations「非難」 **Duchess of Sussex**「サセックス公爵夫人」 **security**「(身辺) 警備；セキュリティ；護衛」 **O. Winfrey**「オプラ・ウィンフリー〈アメリカのトーク番組オプラ・ウィンフリー・ショー (*The Oprah Winfrey Show*) の司会者で女優〉」 **address**「(問題などに) 触れる；対処する」 **recollections**「記憶」 **Prince Philip**「フィリップ殿下〈エリザベス女王の夫。2021 年4月9日に 99 歳で崩御〉」 **Prince Charles**「チャールズ皇太子」 **sweeping it under the carpet**「(問題などを) 隠す；うやむやにする；臭い物に蓋をする」 **crisis talks**「危機管理会議」 **three-sentence statement**「3文の声明〈2021 年3月7日にアメリカで放送されたヘンリー王子とメーガン妃のインタビューについて，エリザベス女王は3文からなる短い声明を発表した〉」 **colonel-in-chief**「名誉連隊長；ボス〈イギリス王侯貴族の名誉職。例えば，バッキンガム宮殿を守る近衛兵の1つであるアイリッシュガーズの名誉連隊長はウィリアム王子〉」 **institution of the monarchy**「君主制という制度」

Exercises

A Listen to the CD and fill in the blanks in the text. CD 35

B Multiple Choice Questions

1. During the interview with Oprah Winfrey, Prince Harry
   a. accused his grandmother of racism.
   b. suggested that his grandmother treated his wife unfairly.
   c. claimed that he and his grandmother have a good relationship.

2. Harry and Meghan are upset because
   a. racist comments were made regarding their child.
   b. their child was not given a royal title or proper security.
   c. both *a* and *b*

3. Buckingham Palace
   a. responded immediately to refute the allegations made during the interview.
   b. expressed sadness to learn that the situation had been so challenging for Harry and Meghan.
   c. cancelled all Zoom calls between the royal family and Meghan and Harry's son Archie.

4. What did **NOT** happen following the interview?
   a. Prince Charles avoided speaking with reporters.
   b. Prince Charles issued a statement praising Britain's diversity.
   c. The Queen issued an official statement through Buckingham Palace.

C Translate the following Japanese into English. Then listen to the CD and practice the conversation with your partner.　◉ CD 36

A: Did you see the interview with Oprah? Talk about explosive!

B: Of course! ¹. _____ . I feel so sorry for Queen Elizabeth.

A: For the Queen? What about poor Meghan? ². _____
_____ .

B: Didn't you think she was just being dramatic?

A: No way! This was about her son—and the systemic racism at Buckingham Palace.

B: ³. But_____
_____ .

A: The issue is not with the Queen. It's with the institution of the monarchy.

B: Well, let's hope everything gets straightened out quickly.

1. 絶対に見逃すわけがありませんよ。
2. あまりにもひどい状況に，彼女は自殺まで考えていました。
3. でも，女王は，彼らが家族の一員として愛されていることを強調していました。

D Summary Practice: Fill in the blanks with suitable words beginning with the letters indicated.　◉ CD 37

The British (¹. **r**   ) (². **f**   ) is in the news following an
(³. **e**   ) (⁴. **i**   ) with (⁵. **O**   )
Winfrey during which (⁶. **a**   ) of racism were made.
Prince Harry and his wife, (⁷. **M**   ) Markle, sat down with the
talk show (⁸. **h**   ) to discuss their grievances with life in the
(⁹. **m**   ), including lack of (¹⁰. **s**   ) and a
(¹¹. **t**   ) for their young son (¹². **A**   ) and even disturbing
comments about (¹³. **r**   ) from an (¹⁴. **u**   ) family
member. On the other side of the ocean, the monarchy began (¹⁵. **c**   )
talks, with Prince Charles (¹⁶. **d**   ) questions about the
interview. (¹⁷. **F**   )-(¹⁸. **e**   ) hours after the bombshell show,
the Queen issued a statement saying the whole family was
(¹⁹. **s**   ) to learn of the difficulties they had faced and
assuring that the matter would be investigated (²⁰. **s**   ) and
(²¹. **p**   ).

E Discussion: Share your ideas and opinions with your classmates.

1. How much do you know about the British royal family? Try to draw a family tree beginning with Queen Elizabeth. Who are the next five people in line to the throne?

2. Do an internet search to find more information about either Queen Elizabeth, Prince Harry or his wife Meghan Markle.

3. What are some differences and some similarities between the British and Japanese royal families? Can you imagine a similar situation occurring in Japan? Why or why not?

News Story 13

First Pilot to Break the Sound Barrier

GRANGER/Jiji Press Photo

Before You Watch the News

Air Date: December 8, 2020
Duration: 1′ 36″

Preview Questions

1. Who was America's greatest pilot?

——アメリカで最も偉大なパイロットとは誰のことですか。

2. Why was he considered to be so great?

——なぜ彼はそれほど偉大だと考えられていましたか。

Warm-up Exercises

A Vocabulary Check: Choose the correct definition for each of the words below.

1. enlist （　）

2. mechanic （　）

3. verge （　）

4. exceed （　）

5. ace （　）

a. to be greater in number or size than

b. to join the armed services

c. a master; an expert

d. a person who maintains and repairs machinery

e. edge

B Fill in the blanks with appropriate expressions from the Vocabulary Check above. Change the word forms where necessary.

1. Have you been able to find a (   ) to work on your Italian sports car?

2. Among all our batters, Tom is our (   ) this season. We know we can count on him!

3. We were told that the total cost of the project should not (   ) $500.

4. Jan's brother (   ) in the Navy right after high school.

5. I can't stop working yet! I'm on the (   ) of a breakthrough.

News Story [1′ 36″]

D. Muir: Finally tonight here, America's greatest pilot.

Retired Air Force Brigadier General Chuck Yeager was born in Myra, West Virginia, in 1923. Enlisting at 18 years old, he was an airplane mechanic, and then a fighter pilot in World War II. And
1. _____, October 14th, 1947… 5

Reporter: The pilot, Captain Chuck Yeager.

D. Muir: …Chuck Yeager was on the verge of history. 10

Reporter: The X1 becomes airborne on its first attempt to exceed the speed of sound.

D. Muir: Attempting to fly faster than the speed of sound.

Reporter: Captain Charles Yeager 2. _____
_____ of the rocket craft. 15

D. Muir: Piloting a Bell X1 research aircraft taken up in a B-29 bomber. The drop.

Reporter: Drop. The ace in the sky drops clear.

D. Muir: [3.] _____

_____.

Reporter: With all four rockets firing, Yeager climbs to 56,000 feet.

D. Muir: And then, the moment.

Reporter: He does it. The first human to crack the sound barrier.

D. Muir: Reaching a speed of 700 miles an hour and [4.] _____

_____.

Reporter: This flight marks the first milestone in the supersonic chapter in the history of aviation. 10

D. Muir: Yeager would serve in Vietnam, and later as the head of Aerospace Safety for the Air Force. And he would break the sound barrier several more times, [5.] _____.

Captain C. Yeager, pilot: What I am, I owe to the Air Force, because it took an 18-year-old kid out of West Virginia and made me what I was. 15

D. Muir: We all celebrate a great tonight. I'll see you tomorrow. Good night.

Notes   **Brigadier General**「准将〈アメリカ空軍などの階級で，大佐（colonel）より上で，少将（major general）より下の位。イエーガー氏は 2020 年 12 月 7 日に 97 歳で亡くなった〉」 **Myra**「マイラ〈ウェストバージニア州西部リンカーン郡に位置するコミュニティ〉」 **fighter pilot**「戦闘機のパイロット」 **Captain**「大尉〈アメリカ空軍などの階級で，中尉（first lieutenant）より上で，少佐（major）より下の位〉」 **X1**「X1 機〈ロケット・エンジン搭載の超音速機で，ベル社が開発した実験機〉」 **becomes airborne**「空中で切り離す（投下する）〈B-29 爆撃機の下に機体を吊した状態で離陸して，空中で母機から切り離した（投下）後にロケット・エンジンを始動する〉」 **rocket craft**「ロケット機」 **taken up in ~**「～から吊された」 **The ace in the sky drops clear.**「空中のロケット機は無事切り離（投下）されました。」 **head of Aerospace Safety**「航空安全局の責任者」 **We all celebrate a great tonight.**「〈= We all celebrate a great *man* tonight.〉」

After You Watch the News

Exercises

A Listen to the CD and fill in the blanks in the text. ⊙ CD 38

B Mark the following sentences true (T) or false (F) according to the information in the news story.

(　　) **1.** Chuck Yeager worked as an airplane mechanic before enlisting in the Air Force.

(　　) **2.** The first time he piloted the Bell X1, Yeager was unable to break the sound barrier.

(　　) **3.** Yeager became famous for flying faster than the speed of sound.

(　　) **4.** Chuck Yeager flew at 700 mph at a height of 56,000 feet.

(　　) **5.** Yeager did several different jobs for the Air Force.

(　　) **6.** Yeager broke the sound barrier for the second time at the age of 89.

C Translate the following Japanese into English. Then listen to the CD and practice the conversation with your partner. ⊙ CD 39

A: Did you hear that Chuck Yeager died?

B: Yeager? ¹. ＿＿＿＿＿＿＿＿＿＿＿＿＿＿＿＿＿＿＿＿＿＿＿

＿＿＿＿＿＿＿＿＿＿＿＿＿＿＿＿＿ , right?

A: For a while, yeah. But that's not why they call him America's greatest pilot.

B: Why, then?

A: ². Back in 1947, ＿＿＿＿＿＿＿＿＿＿＿＿＿＿＿＿＿＿＿＿＿

＿＿＿＿＿＿＿＿＿＿＿＿＿＿＿ .

B: No kidding! That must have been a real milestone.

A: You can say that again. ³. ＿＿＿＿＿＿＿＿＿＿＿＿＿＿＿＿＿＿

＿＿＿＿＿＿＿＿＿＿＿＿＿＿ .

1. 彼は空軍の航空安全局の責任者だったのですよね。

2. 1947 年に，彼は人類で初めて音速の壁を破りました。

3. 彼は，アメリカに新しい科学の時代をもたらしました。

D **Summary Practice: Fill in the blanks with suitable words beginning with the letters indicated.**

⊙ CD 40

At the young age of (¹· **t**   )-(²· **f**   ), Chuck Yeager made
(³· **h**   ) as the first person to break the (⁴· **s**   )
(⁵· **b**   ). Yeager (⁶· **e**   ) in the (⁷· **A**   )
(⁸· **F**   ) at eighteen, working as an (⁹· **a**   )
(¹⁰· **m**   ) and then a (¹¹· **f**   ) (¹²· **p**   ) during
World War II. It was the next act, however, that made him a household
name. Carried into the sky by a B-29 (¹³· **b**   ), the Bell X-1
research (¹⁴· **a**   ) piloted by Yeager reached a height of
(¹⁵· **f**   )-(¹⁶· **s**   ) thousand feet. When the moment came that it
reached a speed of (¹⁷· **s**   ) (¹⁸· **h**   ) miles an hour,
history was made: Yeager had become the first human to (¹⁹· **e**   )
the (²⁰· **s**   ) of sound. In his later years, he served in
(²¹· **V**   ) and had the opportunity to break the sound barrier
several more times—including at the age of (²²· **e**   )-(²³· **n**   ).
An American great, to be sure!

E **Discussion: Share your ideas and opinions with your classmates.**

1. Chuck Yeager's 1947 flight that broke the sound barrier is called a milestone in the history of aviation. What are some other milestones in aviation? What kinds of new aviation-related milestones might we expect in the coming years?

2. Chuck Yeager enlisted in the Air Force at a young age, and credited the organization for making him what he was. What do you think he meant by that? How might the Air Force have changed him? Look for other stories about people who were positively influenced by their experience in the military.

3. In 1983, an award-winning movie about Chuck Yeager's life entitled *The Right Stuff* was made. If you can, watch the film to learn more about this remarkable man.

Biden's Historic Stimulus Bill

Before | You Watch the News

Air Date: March 12 2021
Duration: 2′ 03″

Preview Questions

1. What was the purpose of the bill just signed by President Biden?

——バイデン大統領が署名したばかりの法案の目的は何でしたか。

2. How is it expected to affect the American people?

——この法案はアメリカ国民にどのような影響を与えると思われますか。

Warm-up Exercises

A Vocabulary Check: Choose the correct definition for each of the words below.

1. promote （　）

2. boost （　）

3. furlough （　）

4. game changer （　）

5. crisscross （　）

a. to go around; to cross back and forth

b. to encourage

c. a period of time to stop work due to special conditions

d. support or advance

e. something that causes a big change

B **Fill in the blanks with appropriate expressions from the Vocabulary Check above. Change the word forms where necessary.**

1. The new after-school program will give a (   ) to students struggling with math.

2. Ellie had expected a full schedule for July, but she was put on (   ).

3. That new medication could be a real (   ) for people suffering from allergies.

4. The publisher is strongly (   ) Ben's new book. It could become a bestseller!

5. After completing our research project, we (   ) the desert before returning home.

News Story [2′ 03″]

D. Muir: The Treasury Department has now sent out the first of those $1,400 stimulus checks. About 85% of Americans will get them, part of President Biden's historic COVID relief bill. And now, of course, it's signed into law. At a Rose Garden event today, the president telling American families that, quote, "Help is here." Here's our senior White House correspondent, Mary Bruce, tonight.

M. Bruce: In the Rose Garden today, President Biden kicking off a campaign to promote his historic stimulus plan with a promise **1.** _____ _____.

President J. Biden: To every American watching, help is here, and we will not stop working for you.

M. Bruce: Not a single Republican present at today's ceremony, because **2.** _____.

But outside Washington, the law has broad support. Seventy percent of Americans back it, including 41% of Republicans. The $1.9-trillion-plan gives 85% of Americans a $1,400 check. Those payments starting to hit bank accounts tonight. The law also extends unemployment benefits at $300 a week through early September and lowers health care premiums for millions of

Americans on Obamacare. The airlines also getting a boost, $15 billion, allowing American Airlines and United to tear up furlough notices for nearly 30,000 workers. For flight attendant Brittany Riley, [3.] _____ 10

_____ ,

it's a game changer.

B. Riley, United AFA, flight attendant: I literally felt like there were bricks just lifted off my chest. The biggest sense of relief, knowing that [4.] _____ _____ and focus on... on providing for 15 our family and providing for ourselves.

D. Muir: And so, let's get right to Mary Bruce. She's at the White House tonight. And Mary, President Biden, Vice President Kamala Harris and others hitting the road in the coming week. [5.] _____ _____. They hope to explain how the law, how 20 this relief will help American families and small businesses, and they also know the polling is on their side with this.

M. Bruce: They do. And even though [6.] _____ _____, the president is still making a big sales push. Next week, he and his team will be crisscrossing the country, with Biden himself 25 visiting Pennsylvania and the critical state of Georgia, David.

Notes　**the Treasury Department**「財務省〈= United States Department of the Treasury〉」　**stimulus checks**「景気刺激策の小切手」　**COVID relief bill**「新型コロナウイルス感染症救済法案」　**signed into law**「署名して法律として成立させた」　**Rose Garden**「ローズ・ガーデン〈ホワイトハウス内の庭で，大統領がここで演説することも多い〉」　**stimulus plan**「景気刺激策」　**hit**「（銀行口座に）入る；入金される」　**health care premiums**「医療保険料」　**Obamacare**「オバマケア〈オバマ政権による医療保険制度（改革；法案）〉」　**tear up ~**「～を取り消す；～を破棄する」　**United AFA, flight attendant**「ユナイテッド航空客室乗務員協会所属の客室乗務員〈AFA = Association of Flight Attendants〉」　**bricks just lifted off my chest**「胸の重いつかえがおりた（ようにスーッとする）」　**hitting the road**「（国を横断する旅に）出発する；出掛ける」　**polling**「世論」　**making a big sales push**「売り込みをかける；景気刺激策について宣伝する」　**critical state**「重要な州〈2021年1月5日にジョージア州で行われた2議席をめぐる連邦議会上院決選投票で，2議席とも民主党新人が共和党現職から奪還した。これによって民主党が上下両院の多数党となり，バイデン大統領の政権運営に大きく貢献することとなった〉」

Background of the News

　バイデン大統領は2021年3月11日，新型コロナウイルス感染症対策と景気対策を盛り込んだ「2021年米国救済計画法」（American Rescue Plan Act of 2021）に署名し，同法が成立した。News Story 14では歴史的な救済法案（historic COVID relief bill）として紹介されている。

　財務省（the Treasury Department）が家計の逼迫を和らげるために景気刺激策の小切手（stimulus check）を1人あたり最大1,400ドル配布し，失業給付（unemployment benefits）は，週300ドルを加算する特例措置が3月半ばで期限切れになる予定だったが，9月初めまで延長された。家計向け支援だけでも1兆ドル規模となる。他にも，新型コロナウイルス感染症対策としてワクチン接種の加速のために4,000億ドル，州などの地方政府支援に3,500億ドル，中小企業（small businesses）支援に500億ドルが盛り込まれ，総額1兆9,000億ドル（約200兆円）規模となった。

　民主党系の著名な経済学者らは，2021年3月30日付の『エコノミスト』で，この巨額の財政支出に異論を唱えている。ハーバード大学のローレンス・サマーズ教授らは，バイデン政権の過大な景気刺激策によってインフレが起きる可能性があると主張している。今後，物価上昇が先行すると，賃金の上昇が追いつかずに生活が苦しくなるため，年金生活の高齢者などといった社会的弱者ほど打撃が大きく，アメリカ経済を危機に陥れる恐れがあると警鐘を鳴らしている。

Exercises

A Listen to the CD and fill in the blanks in the text.

 CD 41

B Multiple Choice Questions

1. The new stimulus bill
   a. is intended to support only Americans who are unemployed.
   b. will provide free health care for Americans through Obamacare.
   c. includes checks for about 85% of Americans and support for small businesses.

2. The bill signed by President Biden
   a. currently has the support of the majority of American citizens.
   b. is supported by almost half of Republicans and half the Republican members of Congress.
   c. will hopefully gain the support of the majority of Americans following Biden's big sales push.

3. Which statement is true regarding the stimulus checks?
   a. They are just one part of a larger $1.9 trillion plan.
   b. They will be sent to those living outside Washington first.
   c. The first ones will be sent out after the president's campaign tour.

4. Because of the stimulus bill, some airlines
   a. will be able to hire an additional 30,000 workers.
   b. will be given $15 billion each to avoid bankruptcy.
   c. will be able to bring thousands of employees back to work.

C Translate the following Japanese into English. Then listen to the CD and practice the conversation with your partner. ◎ CD 42

A: It's here! ^{1.} <u>I just checked and</u> _____

_____.

B: That was really quick. What a huge relief.

A: You can say that again. Now if we can get some money for the restaurant, we'll really be in good shape.

B: Haven't you heard? Marty said he's expecting a large check in about a week.

A: That's great news!

B: ^{2.} _____

_____, and he's doing it.

A: Yeah. ^{3.} _____.

B: Me, too. It will be so good to get back to work.

1. いま確認したら，景気刺激策法案からのお金が私たちの銀行口座に入っています。

2. バイデン大統領は、中小企業を後押しすると約束し，それを実行しています。

3. 倒産の危機に直面するのではないかと心配していました。

Summary Practice: Fill in the blanks with suitable words beginning with the letters indicated. CD 43

His historic COVID (¹· **r**   ) (²· **b**   ) now signed into law, President Biden today promised millions of Americans that "(³· **H**   ) is here" in a (⁴· **R**   ) (⁵· **G**   ) ceremony. Backed by (⁶· **s**   ) percent of Americans, the bill includes (⁷· **s**   ) (⁸· **c**   ) for $1,400, as well as extending $(⁹· **t**   ) (¹⁰· **h**   ) a week in (¹¹· **u**   ) benefits through September. Furthermore, (¹²· **h**   ) (¹³· **c**   ) premiums will be lowered for the millions of Americans on (¹⁴· **O**   ). In a lucky break for many (¹⁵· **f**   ) (¹⁶· **a**   ) like Brittany Riley, American Airlines and United will get a big (¹⁷· **b**   ) as part of the new package, allowing them to rescue nearly (¹⁸· **t**   ) (¹⁹· **t**   ) employees from (²⁰· **f**   ). The bill is already (²¹· **p**   ), but the president will be (²²· **c**   ) the country, making a big sales push. For millions of Americans, the relief bill is a real (²³· **g**   ) (²⁴· **c**   ).

E **Discussion: Share your ideas and opinions with your classmates.**

1. How did the Japanese government support citizens during the pandemic? Were stimulus checks distributed? Was there support for businesses? Did most people seem to be satisfied with the support offered?

2. Work with a group of 3 or 4 students. Imagine that you are on a committee charged with finding ways for universities to support students during a pandemic. Brainstorm a list of requests that would make life easier and allow you to better focus on studying.

3. Why do you think Biden's stimulus bill is being called "historic"?

News Story 15

Crisis at the Border

Air Date: March 16 2021
Duration: 1' 44"

Before You Watch the News

Preview Questions

1. What is the current situation at the U.S.-Mexico border?
   ——アメリカとメキシコの国境の現状はどうなっていますか。

2. How is the government dealing with it?
   ——政府はどのように対処していますか。

Warm-up Exercises

A Vocabulary Check: Choose the correct definition for each of the words below.

1. acknowledge (　)
2. brace (　)
3. grapple (　)
4. surge (　)
5. dire (　)

a. a sudden powerful movement or growth
b. extremely serious; urgent
c. to prepare for something difficult
d. to struggle; to clash
e. to accept; to admit

B Fill in the blanks with appropriate expressions from the Vocabulary Check above. Change the word forms where necessary.

1. A young man in the crowd (   ) with the attacker and took his knife away.

2. We were (   ) for the worst, so it was a huge relief to learn that Grandpa was expected to fully recover.

3. If another typhoon hits the coastal area, the results could be (   ).

4. A week after the scandal broke, the mayor (   ) his role in the incident.

5. The sudden (   ) in air travel following the pandemic left many airlines understaffed.

News Story [1' 44"]

D. Muir: And you heard the president there send that message not to come. It comes just hours after his own Homeland Security chief Alejandro Mayorkas acknowledged that they are bracing for more migrants than any time in the past 20 years, but also saying repeatedly today ^{1.} _____ _____. ABC's Marcus Moore from Texas tonight.

M. Moore: The Biden administration tonight grappling with a growing surge of young migrants at the southern border. The Homeland Security chief warning about the dire situation, but he says the border is secure.

A. Mayorkas, Secretary of Homeland Security: This is what we do. We know how to secure the border. We know ^{2.} _____ _____. And we know how to build legal and safe pathways to the United States that the law provides.

M. Moore: FEMA preparing to welcome up to 3,000 unaccompanied migrant teen boys at this downtown Dallas convention center. Still, despite the message to migrants calling for patience and not to come now, DHS says it expects the surge to continue, ^{3.} _____

_____ than in the past 20 years and in the middle of a pandemic.

Sources say the number of unaccompanied children under the age of 18 in Border Patrol custody

5

jumped 25% in just the last week. And because of the lag in the transfer process to the U.S. Refugee Agency, Mayorkas admitted that at times, some are held longer than the three-day maximum required by law. Our Cecilia Vega was at the southern border and spoke to lawyers who met with children **4.** _____.

10

N. Desai, Director of Immigration, National Center for Youth Law: There were so many young children, and more than that, it was striking that, at least for the ones that we spoke to, that many of them have immediate family to whom they can be released.

15

M. Moore: David, the convention center... center here in Dallas **5.** _____

_____.

Officials hope it will reduce the strain on Border Patrol stations that have been seeing those record increases in unaccompanied migrant kids. David?

20

D. Muir: All right, Marcus Moore, from Dallas. Marcus, thank you.

Notes   **Homeland Security**「国土安全保障省〈= United States Department of Homeland Security (DHS)；2002年に設立されたアメリカ合衆国政府の部門で，テロ攻撃や災害から国土を守るのが目的〉」 **Alejandro Mayorkas**「アレハンドロ・マヨルカス（国土安全保障長官）」 **FEMA**「フィーマ；連邦緊急事態管理庁〈= Federal Emergency Management Agency 1979年に設立された（2003年から国土安全保障省の傘下）大災害に対応するアメリカの政府機関）」 **unaccompanied**「親を伴わない；同伴者のいない」 **Border Patrol**「国境警備隊」 **the U.S. Refugee Agency**「米国難民局〈米保健福祉省（HHS: 正式名称は United States Department of Health and Human Services）を指すものと思われる〉」 **Director of Immigration, National Center for Youth Law**「入国管理局長，国立青少年法センター」

バイデン政権が，移民排斥を進めたトランプ前政権からの転換を打ち出しているため，中米諸国で移民熱が高まっている。2021月7月17日付の『日本経済新聞』によると，アメリカ南部国境（southern border）での6月の拘束者数は18万8829人になり，2020年10月からの累計は111万9204人と，100万人を上回った。バイデン政権発足後，メキシコから国境を越えて入国しようとする人々のうち，保護者と同行していない子ども（unaccompanied children）が急増しており，2021年6月には1万5253人が拘束されたという。

原則として，未成年者は保護者らが見つかるまで，アメリカ当局が認可施設で保護することとしている。未成年者は通常ならば，一定期間内に保護施設に送られることになっているが，このニュースで伝えられているように施設に空きがないため，多くの子どもたちが国境地帯の勾留施設にとどまっている。

不法移民対策を担う国土安全保障長官（Homeland Security chief）のマヨルカス氏は，キューバのハバナ生まれで幼少期にアメリカへ移住した。バイデン大統領は，同氏をヒスパニック系で初めてとなる国土安全保障長官に起用した。

After   You Watch the News

Exercises

A Listen to the CD and fill in the blanks in the text.   ◎ CD 44

B Mark the following sentences true (T) or false (F) according to the information in the news story.

(   ) **1.** The president urged people not to enter the U.S. because of the pandemic.

(   ) **2.** The secretary of Homeland Security is confident that his agency knows how to deal with child migrants lawfully and safely.

(   ) **3.** There has been a 25% surge in the number of unaccompanied children crossing the border in just one week.

(   ) **4.** Legally, unaccompanied migrant children can only be held at the border for up to three days.

(   ) **5.** Some of the young migrants entering the U.S. have close relatives living there.

(   ) **6.** The surge of unaccompanied migrants is expected to end within days.

C **Translate the following Japanese into English. Then listen to the CD and practice the conversation with your partner.** CD 45

A: Check out this news story on the TV. Look at all those kids crossing the border!

B: Where are their parents? Aren't they with their families?

A: That's just it. [1.] _____

_____ .

B: [2.] <u>They reported yesterday that</u> _____

_____ , but

<u>I didn't realize there were so many kids</u>. What will happen to them?

A: [3.] <u>Well,</u> _____

_____ .

FEMA is arranging that.

B: But what about all those other thousands of kids?

A: Mayorkas insists the situation is secure, but it's looking pretty dire.

1. 18 歳未満の同伴者のいない子どもたちが大挙して渡っています。
2. 昨日，過去 20 年間で最も多くの移民が入国していると報道されていましたが，こんなに子どもが多いとは思いませんでした。
3. そうですね，ダラスのコンベンションセンターでは，最大で 3,000 人の 10 代の少年を受け入れる準備をしています。

Summary Practice: Fill in the blanks with suitable words beginning with the letters indicated. CD 46

While his (¹⁻ **H**   ) (²⁻ **S**   ) chief Alejandro Mayorkas keeps repeating that the border is (³⁻ **s**   ), President Biden is urging migrants not to come to the U.S. Mayorkas insists that Homeland Security knows how to properly (⁴⁻ **c**   ) for the children, but also acknowledges that the current number of migrants is the largest in the past (⁵⁻ **t**   ) years. Considering that this surge is occurring during a (⁶⁻ **p**   ), the situation is clearly (⁷⁻ **d**   ). The surge is also creating a (⁸⁻ **l**   ) in the (⁹⁻ **t**   ) process and as a result, sources say that some migrants are being held longer than the (¹⁰⁻ **t**   )-day maximum allowed by law. Mayorkas' organization is receiving support from FEMA, currently preparing to move 3,000 (¹¹⁻ **u**   ) (¹²⁻ **t**   ) to a large facility in (¹³⁻ **d**   ) Dallas. That will hopefully reduce the strain on (¹⁴⁻ **B**   ) (¹⁵⁻ **P**   ) stations—at least for now.

E **Discussion: Share your ideas and opinions with your classmates.**

1. Do an internet search for updated information on the situation at the U.S.-Mexico border. Are there any recent changes in the laws? What is the current policy for dealing with unaccompanied children?
2. Where do these migrants come from? What are some of their reasons for wanting to relocate to the U.S.?
3. What other parts of the world are currently seeing large numbers of migrants? Where are they from? Why are they leaving their home countries?

Pronunciation Hints from the News　　③ "center" の発音

　　"center" /sentəʴ/ の発音は，アメリカ英語では /t/ 音が有声音化して「センダー」と聞こえることがある。/t/ 音が /n/ 音とアクセントのない母音に挟まれると，このような現象が起きる。あるいは，/t/ 音が発音されないこともあり，その場合は「センナー」に聞こえる。"twenty" も，同様に「トゥエンディー」や「トゥエニー」のように聞こえる。イギリス英語では，この /t/ 音を変化させないで本来の無声破裂音として発音される。

— …they are bracing for more migrants than any time in the past ***twenty*** years, …　　　　　　　　　　　　　　*(Crisis at the Border, p.90)*

— FEMA preparing to welcome up to 3,000 unaccompanied migrant teen boys at this downtown Dallas convention ***center***.

　　　　　　　　　　　　　　　　　　　　(Crisis at the Border, p.90)

— Sources say the number of unaccompanied children under the age of 18 in Border Patrol custody jumped ***twenty***-five percent in just the last week.　　　　　　　　　　　　*(Crisis at the Border, p.91)*

— It's a high drive into deep left ***center*** field.

　　　　　　　　　　　　　　　(Hank Aaron: Baseball Legend, p.39)

— We actually had 900 sea turtles that we, that came into the ***center***.

　　　　　　　　　　　　　(Turtles Rescued from the Cold, p.46)

— Overseas tonight, and Buckingham Palace is now responding after that ***interview*** with Harry and Meghan, …

　　　　　　　　　　　　　　　(Queen: Family Saddened, p.71)

Appendix
巻末資料

Map of the Un

CANADA

Washington

Montana

North Dakota

Minneso

Oregon

Idaho

South Dakota

Wyoming

Io

Nevada

Nebraska

❹

Utah

Colorado

California

Kansas

❸

❶

Arizona

❻
New Mexico

Oklahoma

⓭

Texas

Alaska

⓾

MEXICO

Hawaii

ed States

❶～⓭はニュースに登場した都市名で，州名はイタリックになっています。各都市の位置は，地図上に番号で示しています。

News Story 1
❶Long Beach, *California*
❷New York, *New York*

News Story 2
❸Los Angeles, *California*

News Story 3
❹San Francisco, *California*
❺Chicago, *Illinois*
❻Albuquerque, *New Mexico*

News Story 6
❼Fultondale, *Alabama*
Michigan
❽Birmingham, *Alabama*
Colorado

News Story 7
Alabama
❾Atlanta, *Georgia*

News Story 8
Texas
❿Corpus Christi, *Texas*
the Gulf of Mexico

News Story 9
Texas

News Story 10
❷New York, *New York*

News Story 11
Georgia

News Story 13
⓫Myra, *West Virginia*

News Story 14
⓬Washington, D.C.
(the U.S. capital)
Pennsylvania
Georgia

News Story 15
⓭Dallas, *Texas*

99

TVニュース英語とは

1 アメリカ国内テレビニュース英語の特徴

　本書は直接ニューヨークで受信したテレビニュースから素材を選定し，米国 ABC 放送局本社からニュース映像を提供してもらいテキストに編集している。

　ニュース英語は伝えるメディア媒体の種類上，大きく分けて３種類に分類される。第１は新聞，雑誌などに代表される活字で伝えられるもの，第２にはラジオのように音声情報に頼る媒体から提供されるもの，そして第３番目はネットやテレビを介して音声情報と画像情報が同時に供給されるニュースである。ここでは，第３番目のメディア媒体であるテレビ放送におけるニュース英語の特徴を簡単にまとめてみた。ニュース英語というと使用される英語もフォーマルなイメージがあるが，実際には以下で述べるように口語的な特徴も多く見られる。ここで引用している例文は最近の *ABC World News Tonight* で実際使われたものばかりである。

1.1 ニュースの構成
　まず，放送スタジオにいるアンカーパーソンが，そのニュースの中心情報をリード部分で述べ，何についてのニュースであるかを視聴者に知らせる。アンカーパーソンは，ごく短くそのニュースの概要を紹介し，リポーターへとバトンタッチする。次にリポーターが現地からのリポートを，時にはインタビュー等を交えながら詳しく報告する，というのがテレビニュースの一般的なパターンになっている。それを略図で示したのが次の図である。ひとつのニュースの放送時間は割合短く，普通 1.5 〜 3 分程である。

●ニュースの構成

Anchor, Anchorperson

LEAD
INTRODUCTION（放送スタジオ）

リポーターへの導入表現

Reporter

MAIN BODY（現地からのリポート，
インタビューなど）

リポーターの結びの表現

1.2 比較的速いスピード

　発話速度はセンター入試のリスニング問題で平均毎分約 155 ～ 160 語，英検 2 級では150 語前後ぐらいだと言われている。しかし，生の（authentic）英語になると，かなり発話速度が速くなる。英語母語話者が話す速度は，インフォーマルな会話の場合，平均毎分210 語で，速い場合は人によって230 wpm (words per minute) になる。典型的なフォーマル・スタイルの英語である，アメリカ国内のテレビニュース放送（ABC 放送）を筆者が調べたところ，発話速度は平均 163 ～ 198 wpm であることが分かった。生の英語でも一般的にフォーマルな話しことばほど発話速度は落ちてくるが，アメリカ国内用のテレビニュースは比較的速い方に分類される。

1.3 不完全文の多用

　テレビニュース英語では，be 動詞や主語，動詞が省略された「不完全文」が多く，端的で箇条書き的な表現が好んで使われる。例えば，以下の例は ABC 放送で実際に使用されていた文である。これらは散列文（loose sentence）として，書きことばでは非文とされるが，テレビニュース英語ではよく現れる不完全文の一例と考えられる。

— Tonight, fears the U.S. is on the brink of an outbreak among the birds.

　上記を補足的に書き換えると以下のようになる。
— Tonight, [there are] fears [that] the U.S. is on the brink of an outbreak [of bird flu] among the birds.

　次は，シェイクスピアが人気があることを伝えるニュースからの例である。
— Four hundred years, 20 generations and still going strong.

　これを，説明的に補足すれば，以下のようになる。
— Four hundred years [or] 20 generations [have passed since he died and he is] still going strong.

　新聞英語の見出しでは be 動詞が省略されることはよく知られているが，テレビニュース英語では，主語・一般動詞・be 動詞・関係代名詞などを省略し，箇条書き的な文体で情報を生き生きと伝える。文法より，伝達する意味内容を重視するため，短い語句をたたみかけるように次々つなぐのである。特に，ニュースの冒頭部分で何についての報道であるか，そのトピックを告げるときにこの文体はよく用いられる。以下の（∧）は，そこに何らかの項目が省略されていることを示している。

— ∧ Sixty-nine years old, ∧ married for 35 years, ∧ lives in Honolulu.
— The weather was calm, the tide ∧ high, ...
— This is the fifth anniversary of the Columbine tragedy, ∧ the worst school shooting in U.S. history.
— Today, ∧ the battle for Ohio.

このような不完全文を使うことによって，ニュースに緊張感や臨場感を持たせ，視聴者の興味を引き付けている。テレビニュースの場合は視聴者の視覚に訴える画像情報があるので，完全で説明的な文体を使用するよりは，むしろ箇条書的な不完全文の方が視聴者にアピールしやすい。

1.4 現在時制が多い

最新のニュースを伝えるというテレビニュースの即時性を考えれば，現在形や近い未来を表す表現が多いことは容易に予想される。米 ABC 放送のニュースにおける時制について調べたところ，現在形と現在進行形で 46% を占めていることが分かった。現在形や進行形の多用は臨場感を生み出す。

— The world's largest carmakers say they **are going to** lower the frame on sport utility vehicles...

— ..., and Rome's police **are** aggressively **enforcing** the new law, ...

— Americans now **spend** more time on the job than workers in any other developed country.

— ...their budget shortfalls **are** so severe they **are going** to raise taxes.

— Now AmeriCorps **is telling** future volunteers there may be no place for them.

新聞などの書きことばにおけるニュース英語では, 未来を表すのに "be expected to", "be scheduled to", "be to" などやや固い表現がよく使われるが，口語的なニュース英語では "will" が好んで使用される。

— In this crowd, there are damning claims that she is being starved, that she **will** suffer.

— For now, some colleges **will** ignore scores for the new writing section, ...

1.5 伝達動詞は say が多い

ニュース英語の特徴として「誰々がこう言った，何々によればこういうことである」といった構文が多く現れる。主語＋伝達動詞＋（that）節という構文では，伝達動詞は say が圧倒的に多く用いられる。構文に変化を付けるために，主節が文中に挿入されたり、文尾に後置されたりする場合も多い。

— One result of higher temperatures, **says** the government, is more extremes in the weather, ...

— But that's the male reaction, **say** the researchers.

直接話法では，Mary said to Cathy, "I like your new car." というように，「発言者＋伝達動詞」が被伝達部に先行するのが一般的である。ニュースの英語では，このような直接話法を使って「…が〜と言いました」という表現はよく見られるが，以下のように「発言者＋伝達動詞」が被伝達部の後に出てくる場合も多い。また，以下の冒頭例のように，発言

者が人称代名詞以外の名詞であれば，伝達動詞が先に来る。

— "It turns out they're a lot more like people than we thought," **says** the director of the
　 Wolong reserve.
— "I'm going to use an expression," he **says**.
— "It's strange to be here," he **says**.
— "Soon, we're planning to fly from Baghdad to Europe," he **says**.

1.6 縮約形の多用

　以下のような指示代名詞，人称代名詞や疑問代名詞の後の be 動詞，助動詞の縮約形
（contraction）がよく使われる：it's, that's, we'll, don't, I'm, you're, here's, they're, we're,
we've, can't, won't, what's.

　縮約形はくだけた会話英語の特徴である。以下の例からも分かるように，テレビニュー
ス英語では新聞英語とは異なって，縮約形の使用によりインフォーマルな雰囲気が出てい
る。書きことばの原稿をただ読み上げるのではなくて，視聴者にとって親しみやすい響き
を与える口語的なスタイルが心がけられている。

— And the reason why, George, is **they've** learned that the Made in the USA tag carries
　 real weight in China.
— **It's** been decades since then, but polio is still very much alive.
— Add it all up and America's happiest person **isn't** Tom Selleck, **it's** Alvin Wong.
— ..., the one that comes when you **can't** put down the Blackberry or iPhone at home, ...
— **She's** constantly juggling his needs and those of the Cincinnati ad agency she works
　 for.

2　テレビニュースの表現

2.1 冒頭部分の特徴

　ストーリーの全体を予想させたり，ニュース内容に期待を持たせたりするために，ニュー
スの冒頭には短いインパクトのある表現や，やや大げさな表現が置かれる。以下の例は気
球に乗って初めて世界一周に成功した人のニュースである。

— **History was made today** above the Sahara Desert — man, for the first time, has flown
around the world nonstop in a balloon.

　新聞英語では，冒頭の文（lead）で読者の注意をひきつけるために，書き方が工夫され
ることが多い。テレビニュース英語でも，新しいニュースの始まりの部分では疑問文，繰
り返し，文法的に不完全な文などを用いて視聴者の興味をひきつけようとする。

— Finally this evening, *not just another pretty face*.

— *The weather, the weather, always the weather.*

— Finally, this evening, *will they turn the panda cam back on again?*

2.2 リポーター紹介の表現

　アンカーパーソンがニュースの主要情報を紹介した後，リポーターにバトンタッチする時の表現である。日本語のニュースでは「では，現場の〜がリポートします」に当たる部分で，次のように様々なバリエーションがある。

— And tonight, Dr. Richard Besser takes us to a remote part of the world, ...

— ABC's Abbie Boudreau is in Provo, Utah.

— It's a duel in the Capitol Hill cafeteria and Jon Karl explains.

— We asked Bianna Golodryga to find out.

— Lisa Stark explains why.

— Here's John Berman on health, wealth and birth order.

— Jim Avila is at a McDonald's in Newark, New Jersey, tonight. Jim?

　アンカーパーソンが，現場のリポーターや別の放送スタジオにいるニューズキャスターを呼び出す時には，その人にファーストネームで呼びかける。呼びかけられた人は，自分の読む原稿が終了して元のアンカーパーソンに戻したい時にもまたファーストネームで呼びかける。名前の呼び合いがバトンタッチの合図にもなっている。

— **D. Sawyer:** Jim Avila is at a McDonald's in Newark, New Jersey, tonight. *Jim?*

— **J. Avila:** Well, *Diane*, in this one McDonald's alone, more than 1,000 people applied for what's likely to be four jobs.

— **J. Karl:** ..., it's probably going to last in a landfill somewhere for thousands and thousands of years. *Diane?*

— **D. Sawyer:** Okay, *Jon*. That was one sad spoon earlier.

2.3 リポーターの結びの表現

　リポーターは現場からの報道の最後を決まりきった表現で結ぶ。リポーターの名前，放送局，リポート地が告げられる。それぞれの間にポーズを入れ，すこしゆっくり目に言われるのが共通した特徴である。

— John Berman, ABC News, New York.

— Lisa Stark, ABC News, Washington.

— Barbara Pinto, ABC News, Chicago.

— Jeffrey Kofman, ABC News, Nairobi.

2.4 ニュースとニュースのつなぎ表現

ひとつのニュースから別のニュースに移行する時，何らかのシグナルがある方が視聴者としても分かりやすい。後続のニュース内容に応じた様々な表現を使って新しいニュースの始まりを合図している。

— *And finally tonight,* what makes someone the happiest person in America?

— *Now to a story about* the struggle between technology and family time.

— *And finally,* our "Person of the Week."

— *And now, we move on to* an incredible scene across the country today beneath the iconic symbol of corporate America, McDonald's.

— *Tonight,* we want to tell you about something new in the use of brain surgery to control tremors from a number of causes.

2.5 コマーシャル前のつなぎの表現

コマーシャルの間にチャンネルを変えられないよう，次のニュースの予告をする際，以下のような様々な工夫した表現が使われる。

— And when we come back, a master class in enduring crisis from the Japanese people.

— And coming up next, what's become one of those annual rites of spring.

— When we come back here on the broadcast tonight, we switch gears and take a look at this.

2.6 番組終了時の表現

その日のニュース番組は，挨拶や次回の予告などで終わる。

— And be sure to watch "Nightline" later on tonight. Our co-anchor Bill Weir is here — right here in Japan, as well.

— And we'll see you back here from Japan tomorrow night. Until then we hope you have a good night at home in the United States.

— And that's it from us for now.

最近のTVニュースに現れた略語

▼A

AAA	[Automobile Association of America] 全米自動車連盟	
AARP	[American Association of Retired Persons] 全米退職者協会	
ABA	[American Bar Association] 米国弁護士協会	
ABC	[American Broadcasting Companies] ABC放送	
ABC	[American-born Chinese] アメリカ生まれの中国人	
ACA	[Affordable Care Act] 医療費負担適正化法	
ACLU	[American Civil Liberties Union] 米国自由人権協会	
ACT	[American College Test] 米大学入学学力テスト	
ADHD	[attention-deficit hyperactivity disorder] 注意欠陥・多動性障害	
AI	[artificial intelligence] 人工知能	
AIDS	[acquired immune deficiency syndrome] 後天性免疫不全症候群	
AMA	[American Medical Association] 米国医師会	
ANC	[African National Congress] アフリカ民族会議	
AOL	[America Online] アメリカ・オンライン：アメリカのパソコン通信大手	
AP	[Associated Press] AP通信社：アメリカ最大の通信社	
ASEAN	[Association of Southeast Asian Nations] アセアン；東南アジア諸国連合	
ATF	[Federal Bureau of Alcohol, Tobacco and Firearms] アルコール・たばこ・火器局［米］	
ATM	[automated teller (telling) machine] 現金自動預け払い機	
AT&T	[American Telephone and Telegraph Corporation] 米国電話電信会社	
ATV	[all-terrain vehicle] オフロードカー	

▼B

BART	[Bay Area Rapid Transit] バート：サンフランシスコ市の通勤用高速鉄道	
BBC	[British Broadcasting Corporation] 英国放送協会	
BSA	[Boy Scouts of America] 米国ボーイ・スカウト	
BYU	[Brigham Young University] ブリガム・ヤング大学	

▼C

CBO	[Congressional Budget Office] 連邦議会予算局	
CBS	[Columbia Broadcasting System]（米国）コロンビア放送会社	
CCTV	[China Central Television] 国営中国中央テレビ	
CDC	[Centers for Disease Control and Prevention] 疾病対策センター［米］	
CEO	[chief executive officer] 最高経営役員	
CHP	[Department of California Highway Patrol] カリフォルニア・ハイウェイ・パトロール	
CIA	[Central Intelligence Agency] 中央情報局［米］	

CNN　　　[Cable News Network] シー・エヌ・エヌ

COLA　　[cost-of-living adjustment] 生活費調整

COO　　　[chief operating officer] 最高執行責任者

COVID-19　[coronavirus disease 2019] 新型コロナウイルス感染症

CPSC　　[(U.S.) Consumer Product Safety Commission] 米消費者製品安全委員会

CT　　　　[computerized tomography] CTスキャン；コンピュータ断層撮影

▼D

DC　　　　[District of Columbia] コロンビア特別区

DHS　　　[Department of Homeland Security] 国土安全保障省［米］

DJIA　　　[Dow Jones Industrial Average] ダウ（ジョーンズ）工業株30種平均

DMV　　　[Department of Motor Vehicles] 自動車局：車両登録や運転免許を扱う

DMZ　　　[Demilitarized Zone] 非武装地帯

DNA　　　[deoxyribonucleic acid] デオキシリボ核酸：遺伝子の本体

DNC　　　[Democratic National Committee] 民主党全国委員会

DOD　　　[Department of Defense] アメリカ国防総省

DOJ　　　[Department of Justice] 司法省［米］

DPRK　　[Democratic People's Republic of Korea] 朝鮮民主主義人民共和国

DST　　　[Daylight Saving Time] サマータイム；夏時間

DVD　　　[digital versatile disc] ディーブイディー：大容量光ディスクの規格

DWI　　　[driving while intoxicated] 酒酔い運転；酒気帯び運転

▼E

EDT　　　[Eastern Daylight (saving) Time] 東部夏時間［米］

EF-Scale　[Enhanced Fujita scale] 改良（拡張）藤田スケール：竜巻の強度を表す6段階
　　　　　　の尺度

EMS　　　[European Monetary System] 欧州通貨制度

EPA　　　[Environmental Protection Agency] 環境保護庁［米］

ER　　　　[emergency room] 救急処置室

ES cell　[embryonic stem cell] ES細胞；胚性幹細胞：あらゆる種類の組織・臓器に分化
　　　　　　できる細胞

EU　　　　[European Union] 欧州連合

EV　　　　[electric(al) vehicle] 電気自動車

▼F

FAA　　　[Federal Aviation Administration] 連邦航空局［米］

FBI　　　[Federal Bureau of Investigation] 連邦捜査局［米］

FCC　　　[Federal Communications Commission] 連邦通信委員会［米］

FDA　　　[Food and Drug Administration] 食品医薬品局［米］

FEMA　　[Federal Emergency Management Agency] 連邦緊急事態管理局［米］

FIFA　　　[Federation of International Football Associations (Fédération Internationale de

Football Association)] フィーファ；国際サッカー連盟

FRB	[Federal Reserve Bank] 連邦準備銀行 ［米］	
FRB	[Federal Reserve Board] 連邦準備制度理事会 ［米］	
FTC	[Federal Trade Commission] 連邦取引委員会 ［米］	
FWS	[Fish and Wildlife Service] 魚類野生生物局 ［米］	

▼G

G8	[the Group of Eight] 先進（主要）８カ国（首脳会議）
G-20	[the Group of Twenty (Finance Ministers and Central Bank Governors)] 主要20カ国・地域財務相・中央銀行総裁会議
GAO	[General Accounting Office] 会計検査院 ［米］
GDP	[gross domestic product] 国内総生産
GE	[General Electric Company] ゼネラル・エレクトリック：アメリカの大手総合電機メーカー
GM	[General Motors Corporation] ゼネラル・モーターズ社：アメリカの大手自動車メーカー
GMA	[Good Morning America] グッド・モーニング・アメリカ〈ABC放送の朝の情報・ニュース番組〉
GMT	[Greenwich Mean Time] グリニッジ標準時
GNP	[gross national product] 国民総生産
GOP	[Grand Old Party] ゴップ：アメリカ共和党の異名
GPA	[grade point average] 成績平均点
GPS	[global positioning system] 全地球測位システム

▼H

HBO	[Home Box Office] ホーム・ボックス・オフィス：アメリカ最大手のペイケーブル番組供給業者
HHS	[Department of Health and Human Services] 保健社会福祉省 ［米］
HIV	[human immunodeficiency virus] ヒト免疫不全ウイルス
HMO	[Health Maintenance Organization] 保健維持機構 ［米］
HMS	[Her (His) Majesty's Ship] 英国海軍；英国海軍艦船
HRW	[Human Rights Watch] ヒューマン・ライツ・ウォッチ
HSBC	[Hongkong and Shanghai Banking Corporation Limited] 香港上海銀行

▼I

IBM	[International Business Machines Corporation] アイ・ビー・エム
ICBM	[intercontinental ballistic missile] 大陸間弾道ミサイル（弾）
ICE	[Immigration and Customs Enforcement] 移民税関捜査局 ［米］
ID	[identification] 身分証明書
IDF	[Israel Defense Forces] イスラエル国防軍
IMF	[International Monetary Fund] 国際通貨基金

Inc.	[~ Incorporated] 〜会社；会社組織の；有限会社
INS	[Immigration and Naturalization Service] 米国移民帰化局
IOC	[International Olympic Committee] 国際オリンピック委員会
IPCC	[Intergovernmental Panel on Climate Change] 気候変動に関する政府間パネル
IQ	[intelligence quotient] 知能指数
IRA	[Irish Republican Army] アイルランド共和軍
IRS	[Internal Revenue Service] 内国歳入庁［米］
ISIS	[Islamic State of Iraq and Syria] イスラム国
IT	[information technology] 情報テクノロジー；情報技術
IUCN	[International Union for Conservation of Nature (and Natural Resources)] 国際自然保護連合

▼J

JCAHO	[Joint Commission on Accreditation of Healthcare Organizations] 医療施設認定合同審査会［米］
JFK	[John Fitzgerald Kennedy] ケネディー：アメリカ第35代大統領

▼L

LA	[Los Angeles] ロサンゼルス
LED	[light-emitting diode] 発光ダイオード
LLC	[limited liability company] 有限責任会社
LNG	[liquefied natural gas] 液化天然ガス

▼M

M&A	[merger and acquisition] 企業の合併・買収
MADD	[Mothers Against Drunk Driving] 酒酔い運転に反対する母親の会［米］
MERS	[Middle East Respiratory Syndrome (coronavirus)] マーズコロナウイルス
MLB	[Major League Baseball] メジャー・リーグ・ベースボール［米］
MMR	[measles-mumps-rubella vaccine] MMRワクチン：はしか，おたふく風邪，風疹の３種混合の予防接種
MRI	[magnetic resonance imaging] 磁気共鳴映像法
MVP	[most valuable player] 最高殊勲選手；最優秀選手

▼N

NAFTA	[North Atlantic Free Trade Area] ナフタ；北大西洋自由貿易地域
NASA	[National Aeronautics and Space Administration] ナサ；航空宇宙局［米］
NASCAR	[National Association for Stock Car Auto Racing] 全米自動車競争協会
NASDAQ	[National Association of Securities Dealers Automated Quotations]（証券）ナスダックシステム；相場情報システム［米］
NATO	[North Atlantic Treaty Organization] 北大西洋条約機構
NBA	[National Basketball Association] 全米バスケットボール協会

NBC	[National Broadcasting Company]	NBC放送
NCAA	[National Collegiate Athletic Association]	全米大学体育協会
NCIC	[National Crime Information Center]	全米犯罪情報センター
NFL	[National Football League]	ナショナル［米プロ］・フットボール・リーグ
NGO	[non-governmental organization]	非政府（間）組織；民間非営利団体
NHL	[National Hockey League]	北米プロアイスホッケー・リーグ
NHTSA	[National Highway Traffic Safety Administration]	幹線道路交通安全局［米］
NIH	[National Institutes of Health]	国立保健研究［米］
NRA	[National Rifle Association]	全米ライフル協会
NSA	[National Security Agency]	国家安全保障局［米］
NTSA	[National Technical Services Association]	全国輸送安全委員会［米］
NTSB	[National Transportation Safety Board]	国家運輸安全委員会［米］
NV	[Nevada]	ネバダ州（アメリカ）
NYPD	[New York City Police Department]	ニューヨーク市警察

▼O

OMB	[the Office of Management and Budget]	行政管理予算局
OPEC	[Organization of Petroleum Exporting Countries]	石油輸出国機構

▼P

PGA	[Professional Golfers' Association]	プロゴルフ協会〈正式には，全米プロゴルフ協会はProfessional Golfers' Association of America（PGA of America）〉
PGD	[pre-implantation genetic diagnosis]	着床前遺伝子診断
PIN	[personal identification number]	暗証番号；個人識別番号
PLO	[Palestine Liberation Organization]	パレスチナ解放機構
POW	[prisoner of war]	戦争捕虜
PPE	[Personal Protective Equipment]	個人用防護
PVC	[polyvinyl chloride]	ポリ塩化ビニル

▼Q

QB	[quarterback]	クォーターバック（アメリカン・フットボール）

▼R

RAF	[Royal Air Force]	英国空軍
RNC	[Republican National Committee]	共和党全国委員会
ROK	[Republic of Korea]	大韓民国
ROTC	[Reserve Officers' Training Corps]	予備役将校訓練団［米］
RV	[recreational vehicle]	リクリエーション用自動車

▼S

SAM	[surface-to-air missile]	地対空ミサイル

SARS	[Severe Acute Respiratory Syndrome] 重症急性呼吸器症候群
SAT	[Scholastic Aptitude Test] 大学進学適性試験［米］
SEC	[(U.S.) Securities and Exchange Commission] 米証券取引委員会
SNS	[social networking service] エスエヌエス；ソーシャル・ネットワーキング・サービス：インターネットを介して，友人や知人の輪を広げていくためのオンラインサービス
START	[Strategic Arms Reduction Treaty] 戦略兵器削減条約
STD	[sexually transmitted (transmissible) diseases] 性感染症
SUV	[sport-utility vehicle] スポーツ・ユーティリティ・ビークル；スポーツ汎用車
SWAT	[Special Weapons and Tactics] スワット；特別機動隊［米］

▼T

TB	[tuberculosis] 結核
TOB	[takeover bid] 株式の公開買付制度：企業の支配権を得るためにその企業の株式を買い集めること
TPP	[Trans-Pacific Partnership] 環太平洋戦略的経済連携協定
TSA	[Transportation Security Administration] 運輸保安局［米］

▼U

UA	[United Airlines] ユナイテッド航空
UAE	[United Arab Emirates] アラブ首長国連邦
UAW	[United Automobile Workers] 全米自動車労働組合
UCLA	[University of California at Los Angeles] カリフォルニア大学ロサンゼルス校
UK	[United Kingdom (of Great Britain and Northern Ireland)] 英国；グレートブリテンおよび北部アイルランド連合王国：英国の正式名
UN	[United Nations] 国際連合
UNICEF	[United Nations International Children's Emergency Fund] ユニセフ；国連児童基金〈現在の名称はUnited Nations Children's Fund〉
USAF	[United States Air Force] 米空軍
USC	[the University of Southern California] 南カリフォルニア大学
USDA	[United States Department of Agriculture] 米農務省
USGS	[United States Geological Survey] 米国地質調査所
USMC	[United States Marine Corps] 米国海兵隊

このテキストのメインページ
www.kinsei-do.co.jp/plusmedia/41
次のページの QR コードを読み取る
直接ページにジャンプできます

オンライン映像配信サービス「plus+Media」について

本テキストの映像は plus+Media ページ（www.kinsei-do.co.jp/plusmedia）から、ストリーミング再生でご利用いただけます。手順は以下に従ってください。

ログイン

ログインページ

●ご利用には、ログインが必要です。
サイトのログインページ（www.kinsei-do.co.jp/plusmedia/login）へ行き、plus+Media パスワード（次のページのシールをはがしたあとに印字されている数字とアルファベット）を入力します。

●パスワードは各テキストにつき1つです。
有効期限は、<u>はじめてログインした時点から1年間</u>になります。

[利用方法]

次のページにある QR コード、もしくは plus+Media トップページ（www.kinsei-do.co.jp/plusmedia）から該当するテキストを選んで、そのテキストのメインページにジャンプしてください。

メニューページ　　　　再生画面

plus+Media トップ　　　メインページ

「Video」「Audio」をタッチすると、それぞれのメニューページにジャンプしますので、そこから該当する項目を選べば、ストリーミングが開始されます。

[推奨環境]

iOS (iPhone, iPad)	OS: iOS 12 以降 ブラウザ：標準ブラウザ	Android	OS: Android 6 以降 ブラウザ：標準ブラウザ、Chrome
PC	OS: Windows 7/8/8.1/10, MacOS X　ブラウザ：Internet Explorer 10/11, Microsoft Edge, Firefox 48以降, Chrome 53以降, Safari		

※最新の推奨環境についてはウェブサイトをご確認ください。

※上記の推奨環境を満たしている場合でも、機種によってはご利用いただけない場合もあります。また、推奨環境は技術動向等により変更される場合があります。予めご了承ください。

このシールをはがすと
plus**＋**Media 利用のための
パスワードが
記載されています。

一度はがすと元に戻すことは
できませんのでご注意下さい。

◀ ここからはがして下さい

4145 BROADCAST
(ABC) 4   plus**＋**Media®

本書には CD （別売）があります

Broadcast: ABC WORLD NEWS TONIGHT 4

映像で学ぶ ABCワールドニュース 4

2022年1月20日　初版第1刷発行
2022年2月20日　初版第2刷発行

編著者　　山　根　　繁
　　　　　Kathleen Yamane

発行者　　福　岡　正　人
発行所　　株式会社　金星堂
（〒101-0051）東京都千代田区神田神保町 3-21
Tel. (03) 3263-3828（営業部）
　　(03) 3263-3997（編集部）
Fax (03) 3263-0716
http://www.kinsei-do.co.jp

編集担当　四條雪菜　　　　　　Printed in Japan
印刷所・製本所／大日本印刷株式会社
本書の無断複製・複写は著作権法上での例外を除き禁じら
れています。本書を代行業者等の第三者に依頼してスキャ
ンやデジタル化することは、たとえ個人や家庭内での利用
であっても認められておりません。
落丁・乱丁本はお取り替えいたします。

ISBN978-4-7647-4145-4 C1082